THE BEST OF
ROCK

THE BEST OF

RoCK

The Essential CD Guide

Alan Clayson

CollinsPublishersSanFrancisco

A Division of HarperCollins*Publishers*

First published in the United States in 1993 by Collins Publishers San Francisco,
1160 Battery Street, San Francisco, California 94111

Text and Design copyright © 1993 by Carlton Books Limited, London
CD Guide format copyright © 1993 Carlton Books Limited
The Essential CD Guides is a registered trademark

Library of Congress Cataloging-in-Publication Data

Clayson, Alan.
    The best of rock : the essential CD guide / Alan Clayson.
        p.   cm. — (The Essential CD guides)
    Discography: p.
    Includes index.
    ISBN 0-00-255338-4
    1. Rock musicians—Biography—Dictionaries. 2. Compact discs—
Reviews. I. Title. II. Series.
ML 102.R6C5 1993
781.66—dc20   93-11546
                                    CIP
                                    MN

Printed in Great Britain

THE AUTHOR **Alan Clayson** is the author of six books on rock, including biographies of George
Harrison and Roy Orbison. He is an acknowledged expert on 1960s music and as a musician has played
with members of the Yardbirds. He has lectured on popular music throughout the United States.

AUTHOR'S NOTE The choice of the artists and albums featured in this book is subjective, but based on
the following criteria: I have chosen not only acts that dictated shifts in musical trends but also those that, if
not necessarily innovative, were popular exponents and typical of some facet of rock. The recordings section
focuses on well performed prototypes of particular styles, and looks at the way each album changed what
existed previously and influenced what came later. I have tried to strike a balance between the documentary
and the recreational; crucially, all selections are meant to be entertaining.

Contents

INTRODUCTION

BEFORE THE BEGINNING

★ ★ ★

North America's Musical Melting Pot

SINCE PUNK'S GREAT GESTURE OF DEFIANCE, NEARLY ALL CULTURE UNDER THE "ROCK" UMBRELLA HAS BECOME ACCEPTABLE TO ADULTS. EVEN BEFORE THE LATE SEVENTIES, ACADEMIA CEASED DISTANCING ITSELF FROM POP IN GENERAL, WHICH GRADUALLY INFILTRATED SCHOOL CURRICULA.

Until recently, you were not encouraged to think of rock as a viable career unless you'd been born into show business. For a boy to become a rock musician was almost the precise equivalent of a girl becoming a prostitute. A strong incentive for even the most ill-favoured youth was the myth that no matter what you looked like, you could still be more popular with young ladies than the average Joe shuffling about in the gloom past the footlights of the bandstand. Up there, you could make eye contact with girls lining the front of the stage. A beatific smile and a flood of libidinous excitement could seal a post-show tryst in the romantic seclusion of a backstage broom closet.

A more sinister pleasure was handed on from the older realms of country and western (C&W), blues and jazz—"starvation music"—whereby a strenuous round of poorly-paid bookings—some hundreds of miles apart—would degenerate into a subsidized boozing marathon from which less strong-minded players would graduate to amphetamines and worse.

Though blues—later, rhythm and blues (R&B)—and C&W were the main points of reference, rock drew artistically from all points of a spectrum that embraced light classical, British folk song and all manner of trace elements in North America's musical melting-pot: Cajun, vaudeville, Appalachian, gospel, bluegrass, showbiz evergreens—and every shade of jazz, particularly when it was transported to the borders of pop via, say, the humour of Louis Armstrong, the orchestral euphoria of Duke Ellington, or the white swing of Woody Herman.

More specific precedents are found in particular discs. Off-the-cuff examples are 'Boogie Woogie Bugle Boy' by the Andrews Sisters, Hank Williams's 'Move It On Over', 'Wild Side Of Life' by Hank Thompson, Tennessee Ernie Ford's 'Shotgun Boogie' and, more obviously, Roy Brown's 'Good Rockin' Tonight' from 1947, plus any number of gutbucket Mississippi and Chicago blues records.

Many of these were products of North America's Deep South where, before the television became a domestic fixture, "musical evenings" were a frequent occurrence in many homesteads —the backbone of the entertainment coming from guitars. Models with Gene Autry on a rearing horse etched on the "table" had been readily available on the Sears Roebuck mail-order catalogue since the early Thirties.

Home-made southern folk music lay at the bedrock of the "western" in C&W. Before the commercial translation of C&W into a late twentieth century commentary on the aspirations of middle America, today's Garth Brooks CD buyer might once have proffered the excuse, "I just had the radio on. I wasn't listening to it".

"Listening to it" used to suggest association with uneducated, bigots—"redneck" descendants of the pioneers, caricatured as clannish, unsophisticated and anti-intellectual Yet Buddy Holly, Roy Orbison, Waylon Jennings, Buddy Knox and P. J. Proby were five of many who first reached a wider public via local C&W radio.

Knox, a Texan, couldn't recall hearing a single recording by a black artist until he visited New York to promote his million-selling 'Party Doll' in 1957. Through the static, however, white listeners might tune in by accident to muffled bursts of what segregationalists heard as "the screaming idiotic words and savage music" on, say, Shreveport's KWKH where Stan the Man's No-Name Record Jive punctuated the likes of the Midnighters' 'Sexy Ways', 'Sixty Minute Man' by the Dominoes and 'Too Many Drivers' from Smiley Lewis—all about sex and all banned from white radio.

Nevertheless, with its blending of cowboy pessimism and Victorian broadness of gesture, what else is C&W but white man's blues? The incorporation of blues into the stylistic arsenal of C&W behemoths like Jimmie Rodgers and Hank Williams was epitomized by an unusual absorption with rhythm, and vocals couched in rural black phrasing and imagery plus an inescapable commitment to the essence of their songs—and it was when outlines

between C&W and black music dissolved further that Elvis Presley was able to venture beyond regional popularity.

He was preceded by a northerner, Johnnie Ray, "the Prince of Wails", whose melodramatic presentation introduced an exhibitionism long prevalent in R&B. A big on-stage moment was when Johnnie piled into his hit cover of the Drifters' 'Such A Night'. Such a whitewashing of an R&B smash for *Billboard*'s mainstream pop charts was always anticipated—if not welcomed—by black recording artists of the early Fifties as it brought their music, through their performances, to a parallel dimension of teenagers with money to waste.

In the early Fifties, some undiluted R&B found its way into the US pop chart, notably in Fats Domino's ambulatory lope—and the sly lyricism of Chuck Berry, who came to be one of rock's most influential figures. His first smash, 1955's 'Maybellene', owed almost as much to C&W for all its springing from a blues environment.

EARLY ROCK

Rockabilly to the Twist— and Beyond

IN 1954, DETROIT'S BILL HALEY AND THE COMETS GOT LUCKY WITH A CLANGOROUS COVER OF SONNY DAE'S R&B RECORDING, 'ROCK AROUND THE CLOCK'. THEY PUBLICIZED IT AND MANY SIMILAR SOUNDING FOLLOW-UPS WITH ON STAGE FROLICS WHICH—SO PAUNCHY, MARRIED HALEY INTIMATED TO THE PRESS—WERE LESS A PLEASURE THAN A DUTY TO APPEASE TEENAGE FANS.

Elvis Presley would make no such apologies when his time came. For a year before the *Ed Sullivan Show* would dare televise him only from the waist up, Presley had been both hated and adored throughout the South. As it would over the Rolling Stones and the Sex Pistols in succeeding decades, so adult blood had run cold at Presley's epic vulgarity that was taken up by the many other "rockabilly" entertainers who flowered in his wake.

Anyone who'd mastered basic techniques could try rockabilly. The core of its contagious back beat was a slapped double bass and slashing acoustic guitar—supplemented later by drums and, perhaps, vamping piano. Over this rudimentary impetus, you could holler more or less any old how as long as you got "gone" enough to lend unhinged sorcery to the simplistic hep-cat couplets about clothes, lust and doin' the ooby dooby with all your might. Presley's unprecedented chart success was the tip of an iceberg that would make more fortunes than had ever been known in the history of recorded sound. By the later Fifties, every region of the globe seemed to have thrown down an "answer" to Elvis. Needless to say, these sprouted thickest in the States where the likes of Ricky Nelson and the more gifted Eddie Cochran mirrored the King's lop-sided grin, "common" good looks and hot-potato-in-the-mouth singing.

Many thought that Jerry Lee Lewis was simply an Elvis who substituted piano for guitar. There were also black Presleys in Chuck Berry and Little Richard; female ones in Wanda Jackson and Janis Martin; mute ones in guitarist Duane Eddy. A bespectacled one, Buddy Holly made up for a deficit of manifest teen appeal with creative talents—not least of which was an ability to compose simple but atmospheric songs tailored to his elastic adenoids. A pair of "ducktailed" brothers called Everly could be visualized as two Elvi for the price of one but the Capitol record company was lumbered with a pig-in-a-poke in uncooperative Gene Vincent—"The Screaming End"—unreliable in the rock 'n' roll market place against smoother certainties of the post-rockabilly scene with its leaning towards lightweight tunes with

Elvis Presley's first disc, 'That's All Right', was a jumped-up treatment of a Negro blues song.

jaunty rhythms and saccharine lyrics. There were vinyl indications too that even Elvis intended to drop raucous rock 'n' roll and get on with lush "quality" material on the premise that rock 'n' roll was just another fad that chanced to be going a bit stronger than the jitterbug or the creep.

This was certainly the case in a backwater like Britain, riven with pragmatic if inhibited copies of US hits by home-grown rockers like Tommy Steele and Marty Wilde. But, as it was in the States, rock 'n' roll was here to stay.

However, as peculiar to Britain as the Teddy Boy—a hybrid of Edwardian rake and Mississippi river boat gambler—was skiffle which was founded on a more sparse instrumentation and even greater primeval rowdiness than rockabilly. Bossing the form throughout its 1957 prime, Lonnie Donegan was, more than Tommy Steele, a British equivalent of Elvis in his vivacious processing of black music for a white audience. If criticized for broadening his appeal, he made skiffle more homogeneously British by merging black rhythms with pub singalong and English folk music.

After skiffle lost its flavour on the bedpost overnight, many switched their allegiance to less-than-pure traditional jazz—which was to undergo such a revival around 1960 that several of its older practitioners—notably Acker Bilk—made the charts. However, most surviving skiffle groups—including many hit-makers from later eras of pop—backslid via wary amplification to playing selections from an increasingly more American UK Top 20 in local ballrooms. These provided a link from youth club bashes to package tours on the "scream circuit", with a recording contract as a far-fetched afterthought.

With internal sources of new material, the Beatles and other self-created beat groups would give tin-pan alley a nasty turn within a few years. In the early Sixties, however, the jobbing tunesmith was an indispensable staple of the record business. In New York's Brill Building, there was even a song-writing "factory" where such stars-in-embryo as Carole King and Neil Sedaka churned out inconsequential but maddeningly catchy doggerel to be whistled by the milkman while the powers that be prepared to market another ditty by reworking the same precept from a slightly different angle.

The US hit parade—and, by implication, those everywhere else—became constipated with one-shot novelties and assembly-line items by insipidly handsome boys-next-door like Bobby Rydell, Bobby Vinton and Bobby Vee. Another sign of stagnation was the high Hot 100 placings of variations on the twist—as much the latest rave world wide as trad had been in Britain alone. Its Acker Bilk was former chicken-plucker Chubby Checker but all manner of unlikely artists, including Sinatra, were releasing twist records. Worse, it wouldn't go away—maybe because you were too spoiled for choice with alternative dances like the locomotion, the madison, the ungainly turkey trot, the mashed potato, the limbo and even a revival of the charleston. Little dates a Sixties film more than a twist sequence, and, to this day, the elderly will slip into it whenever the music hots up at a dinner and dance.

As hot a property in his way as Checker was Phil Spector, a New York producer, famous for his spatial "wall of sound" technique. Styling himself "the Svengali of Sound", Spector remains best known for hits with two beehive-and-net-petticoat vocal groups, the Crystals and the Ronettes.

Other noteworthy Top 10 newcomers included Roy Orbison with his hillbilly operatic pitch, and Gene Pitney who warped his polished tenor to an incomparable dentist-drill whine. At the latter end of the 3-year hiatus from 1960 came California's Beach Boys who, with their rivals, Jan and Dean, ruled celebrated surfing and its companion sport, hot-rod racing, with a rock 'n' roll chug overlaid with breathtaking chorale. Like Orbison, Pitney and few others from this period, the Beach Boys proved sturdy enough to outlast the prettiest Bobby.

THE BEAT BOOM

Merseybeat

The Kinks' first two singles, 'Long Tall Sally' and 'You Still Want Me', were ersatz Merseybeat.

WITH 1962'S 'TELSTAR', THE QUINTESSENTIAL BRITISH INSTRUMENTAL, THE TORNADOS TOPPED THE US HOT 100 WHERE NO LIMEY GROUP HAD EVER MADE MUCH HEADWAY. IN THE UK, PUPPYISH US BOBBIES WERE NOT AS EASILY HOISTING THEIR DISCS ABOVE NUMBER 20.

None the less, though Cliff Richard's backing quartet, the Shadows, ruled 1962's spring chart with 'Wonderful Land', their reliance on banks of violins bolstered record moguls' theories that outfits with electric guitars were passé even if there was now a swing towards beat groups without a "featured singer" as a credible means of both instrumental and vocal expression.

Some of these groups had been toughened by hundreds of hours on stage in German clubs. Among these were the Beatles, the Searchers and similar Merseyside ensembles who infused their shared repertoires with a grinning Scouse vibrancy. A main reason why the Beatles found themselves the figureheads of the beat boom was the formidable songwriting partnership of John Lennon and Paul McCartney—though few London recording managers thought that anyone wanted to hear home-made songs. None could foresee that native units, many of them penning their own material, would be leaping up the charts by 1963. Beginning with Merseybeat, Britain would be a nation in which nearly every region was deemed to have a "sound". This figment of publicists' imaginations had germinated during the summer of 1963 when simple

commercial expediency sent even the slowest-witted London talent scout up north to plunder the musical gold.

Gutted of its major talents, Merseybeat was left to rot as the contract-waving host turned southwards to sign up Kent's Bern Elliott and the Fenmen, the Nashville Teens from Surrey and other experienced local acts, as the focus gradually narrowed once more on the capital. Most of those fortunate enough to make the charts went off the boil within a year but the beat boom set new commercial and artistic standards for all pop groups.

By 1964, Lennon and McCartney could afford to toss spare hit songs to others, among them the Rolling Stones. The Stones' unkempt appearance was so vehemently derided by adults that, naturally, they were worshipped by the young. Neither did the group compromise with its music—music that had fermented in the specialist blues venues around London. Among others who patronized these places had been future Kinks, Yardbirds, Manfred Manns and Pretty Things—all poised to breach the UK Top 20 within months of the Stones' first Number 1, 'It's All Over Now'.

Though far from the juke joints of black America, other UK groups like the Downliners Sect, the Animals and the Spencer Davis Group would also try to emulate the Muddy Waters, John Lee Hookers and Howlin' Wolfs of this world but they'd sometimes look and sound dangerously like pop groups. Straying from their blues core, the Yardbirds pioneered extended improvisation and, like the Pretty Things and others, had the nerve to suck Chuck Berry into the vortex of blues, giving credence to trad jazz trumpeter Kenny Ball's jaded opinion that British R&B was just "rock and roll with a mouth organ". Certainly it mined less confining seams than those of older performers like Alexis Korner, John Mayall and Graham Bond, in whose outfits lay future personnel of Fleetwood Mac, Cream, Colosseum, Free and other acts that caught the tide in the second wave of British blues in the later Sixties.

Of a lower caste than the middle class bohemians of the blues clubs, "Mods" preferred "soul" music. Though their records were plugged heavily on pirate radio, genuine US articles like Lee Dorsey, Otis Redding and, especially, James Brown appeared irregularly in Britain. Therefore, Mods made do with groups augmented with horn sections and keyboards, led by such as Cliff Bennett, Georgie Fame, Zoot Money and Chris Farlowe.

None of these worthy bandleaders was to figure in the first all-British Top 10 in March 1964. A further demonstration that UK pop was now generating vast financial power was what has passed into myth as the "British invasion" of North America. Following exploratory forays by the Beatles and the Dave Clark Five, most of Britain's major pop acts harried the US Top 40 to such an extent that, as Frank Zappa, then in the Soul Giants, said: "If you didn't sound like the Beatles or Stones, you didn't get hired."

Even when the Yanks began striking back in 1965, it was by learning the wild Limey idioms so thoroughly that a lot of US and UK sounds were interchangeable. The hardest blow was dealt by the prepackaged Monkees, thrust together by a US business cabal for a television sit-com in which they played an Anglo-American beat group in artistic debt to long-haired entertainers from an island that only 3 years earlier had been regarded as the furbisher of nothing more than 9-day wonders like 'Telstar'.

PSYCHEDELIC ROCK

The Age of Aquarius

WHEN THE CIVIL RIGHTS MOVEMENT WAS FUSED WITH
FOLK SONG IN THE EARLY SIXTIES, IT WAS LABELLED "PROTEST".
THE FOREMOST EXPONENT OF THE FORM WAS BOB DYLAN UNTIL HE
OFFENDED FOLK PURISTS BY "GOING ELECTRIC" CIRCA 1965.
BY THEN, HE HAD MOVED FROM ANTI-NUCLEAR TRACTS TO RAPID-FIRE
"STREAM-OF-CONSCIOUSNESS" LYRICS THAT WERE JOLTING POP'S
UNDER-USED BRAIN INTO QUIVERING, RELUCTANT ACTION.

The Byrds, Manfred Mann and other groups dipped into his portfolio of songs, and even tin-pan alley hacks put their minds to Dylan-type creations to win the approbation—and cash—of the blossoming hippy sub-culture.

Partly through Dylan, lyrics to later Sixties pop songs became less boy-meets-girl. Epitomizing this were the Pink Floyd's 'Arnold Layne' (a transvestite washing-line larcenist) and the abstract 'A Whiter Shade Of Pale' by Procol Harum—while the Move's 'Night Of Fear', 'Heroin' by the Velvet Underground, and the Small Faces' effervescent 'Itchycoo Park' implied drug experience beyond mere pills and reefers.

The growing lyrical complexity was reflected musically as groups progressed from guitars and drums to effects pedals, mellotrons and nascent monophonic synthesizers. Indeed, one of the reasons the Beatles ceased touring in 1966 was that their output had become impossible to reproduce in concert using conventional beat group instrumentation. Before George Harrison's sitar lessons with Ravi Shankar, Indian raga and deliberately induced guitar feedback had been first absorbed by the Kinks and the Yardbirds. The latter also superimposed Gregorian chant and other eruditions on to their artistic grid but it was the Beatles' expensive and syncretic *Sgt. Pepper's Lonely Hearts Club Band* that intensified the notion of pop as an egghead activity.

The most lasting effect of the watershed year of 1967 was the beginning of a transfer of emphasis from 45s to albums. Previously, the latter format had been a cynical and throwaway display of an artist's "versatility" but of no real cultural value. However, with the Beatles' continuing success, it dawned on record companies that it was a false economy not to allow best selling acts longer time and greater freedom in the studio. The consequent output of many groups betrayed a conscious musical progression with an increasing ratio of album tracks the equal of single A-sides in terms of effort and imagination. Sometimes this policy backfired. The Yardbirds' 'Happenings Ten Years Time Ago', for example, put the tin lid on their chart career. Some considered it an aural nightmare while others shared one pundit's claim that it was "possibly the greatest 45 ever released". Of the same vintage, the Pretty Things's 'Mellowing Grey' was as warm with jarring vignettes of music spliced together to coalesce a half-sung narrative. Wilfully uncommercial, it lacked a discernible melody line as it darted from section to dissoluble section.

Nevertheless, albums by both outfits were well received critically, selling steadily if somewhat unremarkably.

By 1967, other humble pop outfits had become pseudo-mystics, dictating shifts in musical—and social—consciousness. Taking the signals they were given, fans took up meditation, vegetarianism, yoga or whatever else the pop in-crowd were currently "into". Fleetingly, you

were convinced—as arch flower-child Donovan was—that God had seen "all the ugliness that was being created and had chosen pop to be the great force of love and beauty".

During this dawning of the Age of Aquarius, rock passed hastily through its classical period. With lack of a preceding article *à la mode*, combos such as Infinite Staircase, Pneumatic Bliss, Tea-And-Symphony and Iron Butterfly intimated musical insights not immediately comprehensible as sitars whined, tapes looped and the Mothers Of Invention inquired, 'Who Are The Brain Police?'

US acts of this bent entertained at the "be-ins", "freak-outs", "mantra-rock dances" and "love-ins" that were held in the parks and transformed ballrooms around the Haight–Ashbury—"Hashbury"—district of San Francisco, now as vital a pop Mecca as Merseyside had been. Hit singles of 1967 by Eric Burdon, Scott McKenzie and the Flowerpot Men all paid tribute to the "flower power" city from whence sprang big-selling psychedelic albums by such

as Jefferson Airplane and the Grateful Dead.

With the inevitable commercialization of flower power, San Francisco became clotted with drug pedlars, teenage runaways and traffic snarl-ups as curiosity-seekers and weekend trippers kept the freshly sprouted record stores, boutiques and restaurants in profit. By winter, Hashbury was all over.

Supplanted in Britain by slouch-hatted Al Capone chic, airy-fairy flower power turned out to be no more the dawning of the Age of Aquarius than the twist had been.

Some rock acts had been either opposed or insensible to the shifts in stylistic parameters. As demonstrated by 'Purple Shades', a Troggs' 45 concerning "the bamboo butterflies of yer m i n d", o t h e r s adjusted t h e m - selves to psychedelia without really getting the point. Conversely,

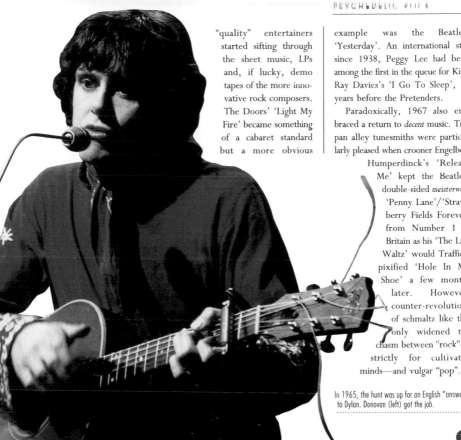

"quality" entertainers started sifting through the sheet music, LPs and, if lucky, demo tapes of the more innovative rock composers. The Doors' 'Light My Fire' became something of a cabaret standard but a more obvious example was the Beatles' 'Yesterday'. An international star since 1938, Peggy Lee had been among the first in the queue for Kink Ray Davies's 'I Go To Sleep', 15 years before the Pretenders.

Paradoxically, 1967 also embraced a return to *decent* music. Tin-pan alley tunesmiths were particularly pleased when crooner Engelbert Humperdinck's 'Release Me' kept the Beatles' double-sided *meisterwerk* 'Penny Lane'/'Strawberry Fields Forever' from Number 1 in Britain as his 'The Last Waltz' would Traffic's pixified 'Hole In My Shoe' a few months later. However, counter-revolutions of schmaltz like this only widened the chasm between "rock"—strictly for cultivated minds—and vulgar "pop".

In 1965, the hunt was up for an English "answer" to Dylan. Donovan (left) got the job.

15

POST-FLOWER POWER ROCK

Rock 'n' Roll Revival

"REVOLUTION IS THIS YEAR'S FLOWER POWER"—
SO FRANK ZAPPA WOULD SUM UP 1968 WHEN, WITH VIETNAM
THE COMMON DENOMINATOR, KAFTANS HAD BEEN MOTHBALLED AS
THEIR FORMER WEARERS FOLLOWED THE CROWD TO GENUINELY VIOLENT
ANTI-WAR RALLIES AND STUDENT SIT-INS.

Because they never returned to stage performances, the Beatles were spared having to be "real" musicians in front of non-screaming audiences. In the later Sixties, bands (not groups) that carried any weight were demanding public attention for lengthy "concept" albums, rock operas and other questionable epics that couldn't be crammed into a 10-minute spot on a package tour. Though gadgetry and constant retakes in the retractable spheres of the studio disguised faults while impinging on grit, there surfaced a deeper respect for instrumental proficiency and, on stage, greater scope for extrapolation. Instead of screeching hysteria, there was knotted-brow "appreciation" of guitar heroes like Jeff Beck, Jimmy Page and Ten Years After's high velocity Alvin Lee. Most worshipped of all were Jimi Hendrix—and the overvalued Eric "God" Clapton whose Cream trio was known to improvise a three-verse

blues at triple-*forte* for nigh on 20 po-faced minutes.

Bands with larger personnel tore pages from the book of Jimmy Page's Led Zeppelin who likewise went in for a high-energy blues-plagiarized brutality. These "heavy metal" outfits popped up all over the world with almost the same frequency as beat groups had in 1964.

Tangential to this was a rock 'n' roll revival in 1968 with reissues of 'Rock Around the Clock' and Buddy Holly's 'Rave On' sneaking into the UK Top 50 while the Beatles weathered accusations of regression with 'Lady Madonna', and the Move invested 'Fire Brigade' with an antique Duane Eddy twang. Even "nice little bands" of progressive hue closed their shows with classic rock medleys. Tiring of psychedelia too, the Rolling Stones had dug down to a bedrock of sorts with 'Jumping Jack Flash', their most enduring 45.

The Stones, Traffic and other influential groups had fallen once more under the spell of Bob Dylan whose *John Wesley Harding* album steered pop away from much of the clutter that had masked many essentially banal artistic perceptions, with a production criteria so shorn of gratuitous trimmings that it sounded *au naturel*. *Music From Big Pink* by the Band, his backing group since 1966, was, however, of more insidious impact in its blend of electric folklore matured over years of rough nights in hick dance halls. Dylan himself liked Creedence Clearwater Revival who, sharing his and the Band's unvarnished arrangements and new lyrical directness, were to supersede the Beatles as Top Group in the *New Musical Express* popularity poll of 1971.

On a more acoustic tack, Traffic popularized a trend for plundering traditional material with the Seventies' 'John Barleycorn'. Their arrangement of this English folk air was thought "purer" than that of more recognized folk-rockers Steeleye Span. The Beatles had brought out the Liverpool shanty 'Maggie May' the previous year, but it was 'John Barleycorn' that spurred the likes of the Nashville Teens' 'Widecombe Fair', Alan Price's 'Trimdon Grange

Explosion' (written in 1882) and hit versions of the hymn 'Amazing Grace' by both Judy Collins and—a UK Number 1—the bagpipes of the Royal Scots Guards.

In the States, musicianly acts like Canned Heat and bottleneck guitar virtuoso Ry Cooder had long been turning to *their* national musical heritage too. The former's album collaboration with John Lee Hooker, *Hooker 'N' Heat*, was symptomatic of a tendency for black blues grandees in the evening of their lives to gear their music for a wider forum by reprising their classics with some of the renowned white rock players they had inspired.

Worthy if unadventurous, such albums were often nominated for Grammy awards but any spin-off singles were hardly expected to make the charts—for, though *Easy Rider* might have been its film, the hit song of 1969 was 'Sugar Sugar' by the Archies. The next logical step after the Monkees, these were a cartoon

Led Zeppelin's Robert Plant was once a member of Midlands beat group the King Snakes.

group that idealized the short-haired sir-and-ma'am characteristics of small-town America. Almost as insubstantial were Ohio Express, Crazy Elephant and other faceless acts manufactured as US chart fodder within the walls of Kasenetz-Katz, the New York "bubble gum" organization that knocked out material for the charts with the same lack of artistic pretension as the jobbing songwriters who had once done the same in the Brill Building.

THE SUPERGROUPS

"Endless Meaningless Solos"

As THE DECADE TURNED, IT BECAME COMMON FOR TOP ACTS LIKE THE ROLLING STONES, JIMI HENDRIX AND THE DISINTEGRATING BEATLES TO ASSEMBLE FAMOUS CONFRERES IN THE SAME BOAT TO ADD ICING TO ALBUMS.

With his Traffic then on hold, Steve Winwood pontificated: "Today's scene is moving very much away from permanent groups. The trend is going more in the direction of the jazz scene when musicians just jam together as they please." In tacit endorsement in December 1968 came an *ad hoc* quartet of John Lennon, Eric Clapton, Keith Richards (on bass) and Hendrix's drummer on the hitherto unseen *Rolling Stones Rock 'N' Roll Circus* film.

Clapton had been invited to a less glamorous all-day function in a southwest London warehouse where many of the ablest musical technicians of two continents dissolved outlines between rock and jazz. Among those captured on film was drummer Buddy Miles whose Electric Flag colleague, guitarist Mike Bloomfield, had already been prime mover in a series of less erudite get-togethers in a US recording studio. With the likes of Buffalo Springfield guitarist Steve Stills and Blood Sweat and Tears organist Al Kooper, the edited result, modestly titled *Super Session*, was the best-selling CBS album of 1968.

The clouds parted again on the gods at play when producer Denny Cordell supervised the esteemed cast—including members of Procol Harum, Traffic

and Led Zeppelin—who assisted on the début album of Joe Cocker who had topped the UK chart with an aptly titled overhaul of the Beatles' 'With A Little Help From My Friends'. Further proof of the soundness of this strategy was when Screaming Lord Sutch also summoned renowned accompanists for two albums that each climbed into the US charts.

Sutch had been support act on the first UK tour by Cream who then removed themselves to grander showcases in North America where snow-blinded applause would greet "endless, meaningless solos", sighed Clapton. While stagnating artistically, Cream broke box office records with a farewell concert in 1968.

Clapton and Cream's drummer, Ginger Baker, next merged with Steve Winwood and bass guitarist Rick Grech for a more calculated "supergroup". Called Blind Faith, they were the prototype of most supergroups since. Weeks before their début performance in London's Hyde Park, a letter to *Melody Maker* wrongly fore-ordained "almost Beatle

The Traveling Wilburys. Back, left to right: "Nelson" Harrison, "Lucky" Dylan, "Otis" Lynne; seated, left to right: "Lefty" Orbison and "Charlie T." Petty.

status" for them. Only a miracle could rescue them, even if the media build-up forestalled instant damnation after a disappointing but chart-topping album and a US tour during which audiences went as ape over strings of bum notes as the outfit's few startling moments.

Blind Faith's precedent was followed more gainfully by Humble Pie—whose selling points were ex-Small Face Steve Marriott and former front man of the Herd, Peter Frampton—whose shallow megastardom accrued diminishing returns over 22 US tours. Next up was the "technoflash" pomp-rock of ELP— with former personnel from the Nice, King Crimson and Atomic Rooster—one of the most grandiloquent supergroups of all.

In a lighter vein, Steve Stills's extempore wanderings since Buffalo Springfield ended in a link-up with ex-Byrd Dave Crosby and Graham Nash, late of the Hollies, in the prosaically titled Crosby, Stills and Nash, styled a "supergroup" by the press before they'd sung a note in public. Predictably, they sold many millions of records.

After George Harrison's star-studded *Concerts For Bangladesh* extravaganza in Madison Square Garden, the supergroup idea was to wear thin later in the Seventies with such events as Eric Clapton's trumpeted come-back concert in 1974 at London's Rainbow Theatre with its noisy percussion artillery and glut of illustrious guitarists.

This most fascist of pop cliques reared up again in 1988 with the Traveling Wilburys—George Harrison, Roy Orbison, Bob Dylan, Jeff Lynne and Tom Petty. Their first effort, 'Handle With Care', could only have come from people who'd viewed the world from the cosseted Mount Olympus of stardom since the Sixties.

The chronicle would not be complete without mention of the "super-sidemen"—an ebullient amalgam from Los Angeles' "blue-eyed soul school"—Carl Radle, Leon Russell, Bobby Keyes, Bobby Whitlock and so on. It was as if rock couldn't be done with any other people than these interchangeable session musicians. Some of them made boring albums of their own, the often short sides bloated with "laid-back" arrangements and lyrics that dwelt on "balling chicks", "toking", snorting cocaine and other overworked myths of the rock 'n' roll lifestyle. Underpinning them would be a snappy jitter described as "tight" or "funky". Exchanging smirks across the console, they and their hangers-on were the epitome of that smug, sexist élite of the early Seventies whose only contact with real life out in Dullsville was through managers, runarounds and narcotics dealers.

THE WOODSTOCK GENERATION

"Gimme Shelter"

HALF A MILLION RAIN-SOAKED FANS BRAVED WOODSTOCK, THE OUTDOOR ROCK FESTIVAL THAT, FROM A DISTANCE OF YEARS, WOULD BE VIEWED AS THE CLIMAX OF HIPPY CULTURE. THIS EVENT AND THE ROLLING STONES' DISASTROUS FREE CONCERT AT ALTAMONT—ALSO IN 1969—ENDED BOTH THE SWINGING SIXTIES AND POP'S TURBULENT ADOLESCENCE.

Nearly all the old heroes had gone down. The Yardbirds, the Small Faces, the Walker Brothers, the Animals, the Byrds, the Spencer Davis Group, the Mothers Of Invention, the Dave Clark Five, Jefferson Airplane, the Zombies and, of course, the Beatles, had all either broken up, or were about to break up, leaving a residue of mostly tedious splinter groups, supergroups and solo performers to add to a growing pile. Many bands would reform, but such a possibility was denied the Jimi Hendrix Experience after the death of its leader in 1970—though the Doors struggled on for a while without their late focal point, Jim Morrison.

The last most people would ever see of Elvis Presley would be on stage in a Las Vegas casino in the white garb of a rhinestone cowboy. After Altamont, the Stones luxuriated in St Tropez and tabloid gossip columns. Most of the rest either withdrew from pop altogether or marked time in cabaret or back-of-beyond dance halls where they were displayed as curios from the recent past.

While T Rex, Slade and Alice Cooper made their chart débuts in 1971, these harbingers of glam-rock were conspicuous by their absences on college juke boxes, full of album-enhancing 45s by Humble Pie, Deep Purple, Man, Black Sabbath and other "heavy" ensembles who appealed to male consumers recently grown to man's estate. Also in favour was the pomp-rock of ELP, Yes and borderline cases like Pink Floyd, the Moody Blues, Deep Purple and—laced with grace-saving humour—Holland's Focus. From continental Europe too wafted the icy, Teutonic charm of Amon Duul, Tangerine Dream, Can, Kraftwerk and Neu.

Jazz-rock also scored in sock-smelling university hostel rooms. Though Britain spawned respectable names such as East Of Eden,

Colosseum and John McLaughlin, jazz-rock's truer home was the United States which abounded with the ilk of Weather Report, Return To Forever, the Jazz Crusaders and Miles Davis, who were often castigated for preferring technique to instinct. Most complaints were directed at the polysynthesizers and similarly expensive state-of-the-art keyboards that floated effortlessly over layers of treated sound on jazz-rock (and pomp rock) discs—for, no matter how cleverly utilized, these seemed impassive and gutless against the potentially more thrilling margin of error with "real" instruments.

Rock music acquired a more human element around 1971 when Carole King's *Tapestry* began a sojourn in the US album charts. *Tapestry* was a less self-obsessed example from the early Seventies denomination of singer-songwriters who infested not only student dorms/bedsits but also the Top 40. Reaching out to self-doubting adolescent diarists rather than headbangers, the genre was called "self-rock" if you liked it, and "drip-rock" if, like *Melody Maker*'s Allan Jones in a scathing article, you didn't.

The bland uniformity of most drip-rock executants was another symptom of the post-Sixties doldrums. With all the charisma of a tin of beans, and lyrics that frequently made you embarrassed to be alive, Joni Mitchell, solemn James Taylor, Cat Stevens, twee Melanie or someone like them would utter "beautiful" cheesecloth-and-denim banalities on television specials, open-air gatherings and sold-out stadiums, having captured the general tenor of the bland "Woodstock Generation"—a re-run of 1967 without colour, daring or humour. Its anthem was Simon and Garfunkel's piteous 'Bridge Over Troubled Waters', and its house band Crosby, Stills and Nash, whose perfect harmonies were now enhanced with the high-pitched cantillations of Neil Young. The basic ethos was of being so bound up in yourself that every trivial emotion or occurrence was worth telling the whole world about. On stage, no Mick Jagger cavortings were necessary. All you had to do was sit on a stool, sing to your guitar and beam

a small, sad smile every now and then.

Because some hip names had been printed on one of his LP jackets and he covered a few drip-rock classics, it was even cool to dig an easy-listening Mr Wonderful like Andy Williams, whose chief ability was adapting just

enough of prevailing trends to not turn off older fans.

One trend not investigated by Williams was a form of rock from the West Indies. While ska, bluebeat and further shades of Caribbean sounds were coalescing into the primeval

atom of reggae, Desmond Dekker, Prince Buster and similar upmarket practitioners had enjoyed isolated hits. Yet it was to be despised by most of the so-called intelligentsia, until, via the auspices of Bob Marley, Burnin' Spear *et al*, reggae in the Seventies would outflank even blues as the new "twisted voice of the under- dog" and student disco accessory.

Rivalling Marley and his Wailers as 1973's toast-of-the-campus was New York's Steely Dan—but, after Mike Oldfield's *Tubular Bells* had set the standard, "works" were very much *de rigeur* too. Jethro Tull, Yes and Hawkwind were among many prominent acts who cut albums as a continuous entity, teeming with interlocking themes, links and leit- motivs. These records would leave their marks on the New Age mean- derings of the Eighties and, before that, the classical-rock fusions of bands like Renaissance, the Electric Light Orchestra and glam-rock late- comers, Queen.

John Hiseman's Colosseum strut their stuff at the 1970 Bath Festival.

GLAM ROCK

Glittering Heart-Throbs

THE LOOK HAS BEEN AS IMPORTANT AS THE SOUND IN MANY STRATA OF POP. AS WELL AS THE NARCISSISM OF TEDDY BOYS AND THEN MODS, THERE WERE SHORTER-LIVED FADS IN WHICH CLOTHES AND MUSIC INTERMINGLED.

A craze for Victorian military uniforms precipitated the climb of the New Vaudeville Band's 'Winchester Cathedral' and similar olde tyme whimsy into 1966's hit parade. Previous to this, Johnny Kidd and the Pirates had gone in for nautical stage outfits with galleon backdrop—while Oregon's Paul Revere and the Raiders would, as obviously, don eighteenth-century frock-coats and tights. With each succeeding single after 1968's 'Legend Of Xanadu', Dave Dee, Dozy, Beaky, Mick and Tich would present a different costume drama on British TV's *Top Of The Pops*.

Theatre was also an integral part of the show for such as the Bonzo Dog Doo-Dah Band, Pink Floyd, the Crazy World Of Arthur Brown and Peter Gabriel's Genesis. Ex-art student Pete Townshend acknowledged auto-destructive artist Gustav Metzger as the doubtful inspiration for the Who's practice of smashing up their equipment amid smoke bombs, flashing lights and feedback lament. Fellow Mods the Creation climaxed their act in more two-dimensional manner by splashing an action painting on to a canvas before setting fire to it.

As if in reciprocation, many genuine daubers and other academics were intrigued by pop. Fine art undergraduate Bryan Ferry was to cut his teeth with northeast soul combo the Banshees before forming Roxy Music—and Andy Warhol's sponsorship of New York's decadent Velvet Underground was yet another deliciously sordid tangent to his Pop-Art pot-pourri and media manipulation.

In the hung-over morning after the Swinging Sixties, multitudes demonstrated tacit weariness of

A quiet moment backstage with the Crazy World Of Arthur Brown.

23

heavy metal, pomp-rock and doe-eyed singer-songwriters by scouring junk shops and jumble sales for overlooked artefacts from earlier rock eras to keep the drab Woodstock generation present at bay. A further sign of disassociation from contemporary pop was the popularity of two 1973 films: *That'll Be The Day*, a poignant evocation of provincial England in the late Fifties, and *American Graffiti,* which recreated 1962 in a California town. Attempts were made to arrange and perform the old-fashioned sounds by British Teddy Boy revivalists like Crazy Cavan and Shakin' Stevens. In the US, Sha Na Na, Cat Mother and Flash Cadillac were also carrying a torch for the Fifties.

Along with the establishment of vintage record shops, retrospectives in pop journals and the snowballing of more erudite "fanzines", haphazard cells of archivist-performers became more cohesive. There were also overtures to spent forces like Bill Haley and Little Richard to appear on nostalgia revues. On the cards too were lucrative "British invasion" reunion tours of the States. By acquiring the rights to ancient catalogues, K-Tel and similar conglomerates specializing in reissues triggered album chart triumphs by the repackaged likes of the Beach Boys, Eddie Cochran, the Dave Clark Five and Roy Orbison.

These often nestled uneasily between the latest by mid-Seventies heart-throbs like David Cassidy, the Osmonds and the Jackson Five. Resplendent in outsize bow-ties and half-mast tartan trousers, the Bay City Rollers were hyped as "the new Beatles" and, for several months, "Rollermania" was rampant among UK schoolgirls—but, with the exceptions of Abba and the youngest Jackson brother, none of these sensations shaped up as either new Beatles or new Elvi.

Cassidy vaguely resembled a lumberjack but the dress sense of the rest of them was mildly reflective of the swing back to the cheap glamour of rock 'n' roll, the beat boom and even Kasenetz-Katz bubblegum. In the UK singles charts anyway, Woodstock patched pastels were chic no more: "in" now were sequins, form-fitting lurex, gold lamé, stiletto heels and mascaraed men dressed up like ladies. Top 30 strikes by T Rex, Slade, Alice Cooper and the Sweet heralded the grand entrance—to tidal waves of female screams—of the greater excesses of Gary Glitter, the veritable overlord of what was now labelled "glam rock".

Its three *éminences grises* were Mickie Most, the Chapman-Chinn team—the Stock-Aitken-Waterman of their day—and Glitter's studio partner, Mike Leander. When their respective runs of hits continued with Suzi Quatro, Hello, Mud, Arrows and further new signings, other entrepreneurs got in on the act. The biggest fish to be hooked were the Rubettes, Sparks, Queen and, though UK success was not immediate—Kiss. The Kinks, the Faces, Lou Reed and the Sensational Alex Harvey Band emphasized glam elements that they'd always had. Even former early Sixties chart

Gary Glitter, godfather of glam.

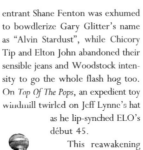

entrant Shane Fenton was exhumed to bowdlerize Gary Glitter's name as "Alvin Stardust", while Chicory Tip and Elton John abandoned their sensible jeans and Woodstock intensity to go the whole flash hog too. On *Top Of The Pops*, an expedient toy windmill twirled on Jeff Lynne's hat as he lip-synched ELO's début 45.

This reawakening of the singles market was accompanied by catchpenny glam-rock albums, padded out with revivals of old rock standards and unoriginal "originals". However, there emerged a new breed of thinking man's glam-rocker in the art-college camp of Roxy Music, which embraced literate compositions and a clever hybrid of kitsch and the avant-garde. Sartorially, members ranged from leader Bryan Ferry's lounge lizard get-up to the androgyny of Brian Eno whose later concerns as a record producer included the diverse extremities of the Portsmouth Sinfonia and Talking Heads. Attracting intellectuals too was David Bowie who, with the New York Dolls, pioneered the undermining of sexual stereotyping. On top of increasingly more flamboyant attire and overtly camp mannerisms on stage, Bowie's public admission that he was bisexual did not finish him—very much the opposite. Soon afterwards, Gary Glitter was kissing his lead guitarist on the cheek, and Suzi Quatro in biker leathers rehashed 'I Wanna Be Your Man' with no lyrical revision.

Whatever its repercussions, glam wasn't destined to last. It was almost exclusively a teenage phenomenon, and both audiences and performers grew up. Yet, for a genre so intrinsically vulgar and fabricated, it is surprising how much scratched glam-rock singles fetch at record fairs, and the extent to which later rock movements were traceable to glam. Furthermore, quite a few of its originators, notably Bowie, Ferry and Glitter, managed to cling to at least an intermittent chart career throughout the Eighties and beyond.

BACK in the USA

Stadium Rock and Disco Fever

GLAM ROCK MADE FAR LESS IMPACT IN THE US HOT 100 THAN IT DID IN THE BRITISH CHART. DURING ANOTHER OF ROCK'S SLOW MOMENTS, THERE WAS IN NORTH AMERICA NO OVERT FOCUS OF ADORATION, NOTHING HYSTERICAL OR OUTRAGEOUS IN 1974.

While precedents were being forged by the likes of the New York Dolls in the city's twilight zone, adolescents and post-psychedelic casualties had to make their own amusements. Woodstock spirituality was forgotten like last year's tie-dyed grandad vest. Cheap spirits, downers, head-banging and streaking all caught on during this apocryphal year.

At roughly the same mental level as such desperate diversions were combos like Rush, the Climax Blues Band, Supertramp and Bachman-Turner Overdrive as well as the better-known "dinosaur bands" lampooned in the music press as either over-the-hill like the Grateful Dead or wholesomely Americanized like Fleetwood Mac. Still, at least they were an excuse for friends to get smashed out of their brains together with the drugs on offer in the toilets, and hurl urine-filled beer-cans stagewards if the band didn't boogie or play the good old good ones in the good old way.

If these squalid entertainments didn't appeal, consumers could turn to what was once the squarest, most right wing subdivision of rock. From the late Sixties, Nashville—the Hollywood of C&W—had been beckoning with greater urgency to purveyors of more generalized pop, albeit of a kind not uninfluenced by country's lyrical preoccupations and melodic appeal. Jerry Lee Lewis would rise anew as a country star, and Elvis would get wise too with 'Kentucky Rain', Tony Joe White's 'Polk Salad Annie' *et al*, either as hit singles or highlights of his Las Vegas pageants.

C&W had started tickling the fancy of a younger audience via albums like the Downliners Sect's *The Country Sect*, the Byrds' *Sweetheart Of The Rodeo* and Bob Dylan's *Nashville Skyline*. Before his death in 1973, ex-Byrd Gram Parsons had discussed with Rolling Stone Keith Richards an even richer blend of C&W and rock for an audience still biased against one or the other.

Taking cues from Nashville's spellbinding gaudiness, its revamped music and the popularity of spaghetti westerns, bars and clubs throughout the globe transformed themselves during the Seventies into parodies of either Wild West saloons or truckers' road houses where conversations would be peppered with

Deep South slang picked up from Merle Haggard albums, C. B. McCall's citizens' band 'Convoy' monologue and country rock standards like 'Okie From Muskogee' and Kris Kristofferson's 'Help Me Make It Through The Night'. Even if these hadn't made the Top 10, they were as well known as many that had.

Kristofferson and Tony Joe White were among a new breed of Southern songwriters considerably less pretentious and artistically self-centred than the Melanies and Neil Youngs up north. From Elvis downwards, their compositions attracted numerous cover versions. Broadly speaking, the milieu was of tougher stamp than the soporific country-rock wafting from the West Coast. Then in vogue were Loggins and Messina, sugary John Denver, Linda Ronstadt and the Eagles whose *Greatest Hits* compilation would be ensconced in the US album lists for most of 1976. Also popular that year and those succeeding was New Jersey's Bruce Springsteen, a singing composer with a Yogi Bear vibrato and energetic stage act that put him a cut above James Taylor.

From just over the border in Philadelphia emanated David Bowie's "plastic soul" album, 1975's *Young Americans,* from which was taken 'Fame', the first US Number 1 for Bowie, whose glam threads had been ditched. Ringo Starr, Roy Orbison and other unlikely rockers also absorbed aspects of the City of Brotherly Love's trend-setting *moderato* style that had put the Three Degrees, the Stylistics and their sort on the musical map. Exhaling from late-night stereos were countless feathery "Philly soul" duplications: all synthesized string backwash, *Shaft* chukka-wukka guitars and a prominent backing chorale lowing an overstretched coda as the main vocalist's hopes of imminent sexual congress increase.

Beyond the mush, "Philly soul" was a key source of chart ballast as disco fever sashayed towards its John Travolta zenith. Moving in fast,

In 1979, Roy Orbison recorded *Laminar Flow*, an album dominated by the *moderato* soul style from Philadelphia.

the Bee Gees metamorphosed from Sixties teen icons to disco paladins when their sound-track to *Saturday Night Fever* filled dance floors throughout the world, selling millions in the process. They'd hired flesh-and-blood musicians for the sessions but their example did little to forestall the rising tide of a synthesizer-processed "bass guitar", soon to yield to the "twanging plank" noise that would plague Eighties rock.

PUNK ROCK

Pistol-Packers and Power-Pop

SEVENTIES POP TENDS TO BE DATED EITHER PRE- OR POST PUNK. IT WAS A REACTION AGAINST THE DISTANCING OF THIS OR THAT REMOTE GROUP—"SUPER" OR OTHERWISE BUT FOREVER IN THE STADIUMS OF NORTH AMERICA—FROM THE CRUCIAL TEENAGE MARKET.

"Why should young kids have to listen to the music their older brothers listen to?" Tommy of the Ramones would ask after his group plus the Shirts, Blondie and other "trash rock" acts surfaced from clubs in the Bowery, the same run-down district that had given birth to the New York Dolls.

The Dolls, T Rex, Lou Reed, Gary Glitter, Roxy Music and other glam-connected stars were among precious few older performers acceptable to punk rockers—the "blank generation"—possibly because "the glam stars were punks", opined Glitter, "but we were a different kind of punk". In Britain, new punk festered initially beneath the "street level" acclaim accorded to "pub rock" performers like Dr Feelgood and Ian Dury who, almost despite themselves, would be swept from the nicotine clouds of bars and clubs and into the Top 40, though, strictly speaking, pub rock as much as trash rock precluded stardom and its isolation from the everyday.

The punk (or new wave) storm broke in 1976 when "radical" pop journalists became evangelical about it via fawning saturation coverage, and toadying to someone called "Johnny Rotten", chief show-off with the Sex Pistols.

It was a fierce time and no mistake. More than rockabilly and skiffle, anyone could do it. As punk fanzine *Sniffin' Glue* elucidated, all you needed were three chords. Not a week went by without another "hot" new wave ensemble ringing some changes and drawing gobbets of appreciative spit from the audience. Somehow, most of them looked and sounded just like the Sex Pistols: ripped clothes, short hair, safety-pin earrings and those three chords thrashed at speed to machine-gun drumming behind a johnny-one-note with a self-denigrating name like "Kenny Awful", ranting against the old, the wealthy and the established.

Thrillingly slip-shod though its aural debris was, punk lacked the musical strength of both the Sixties beat boom and psychedelia. It was always doomed to be ineffectual artistically—and, after the pathetic drug-related demise of Sex Pistol Sid Vicious in 1978 while awaiting trial for the murder of his girlfriend, it had run out of shock tactics.

Following punk in Britain was a hyped craze for "power pop"—

Rot 'n' roll: Johnny and Steve of the Sex Pistols

punk minus the loutish affectations and "revolutionary" message—of which the great white hope was the Pleasers, blue-eyed propagators of "Thamesbeat", who wobbled their moptops and went "oooooo" into a microphone. Then came a resurgence of rockabilly, notably by the Cramps—"psychobilly"—and the Stray Cats, both US outfits.

As it had been with old-style rockabilly, the grubbing show business industry stole punk's most viable ideas and persuaded its more palatable exponents to ease up, grow their hair maybe, talk correct and get ready to rake in the dollars. As his face was his fortune, Generation X's Billy Idol, for instance, was groomed as an updated Ricky Nelson while some of his Generation X colleagues were to form the over-publicized Sigue Sigue Sputnik for a crack at mid-Eighties glam after Adam and the Ants had ruled 1981 with Dave Dee-type dressing-up. By 1986, the Damned had gone smooth enough to score their biggest hit with 'Eloise', lovingly copied from Barry Ryan's string-laden original dating from 1968. In its way, this volte-face was as much the apotheosis of blank generation nihilism as the self-immolation of Sid Vicious.

With one of his songs absorbed into Linda Ronstadt's gooey canon, one of the first British new wave ambassadors to gain tangible success over the Atlantic was a weedy young man in glasses and uncommunicative stage persona with the *nom de guerre* Elvis Costello. Others who used punk as a springboard to greater things included the Police, the Pretenders, Tom Robinson, the Jam and Wreckless Eric, whose Len Bright Combo was to preside over England's Medway towns scene in the mid-Eighties as self-contained in its own way as Merseybeat.

Musically, punk left its mark on a new strain of heavy metal that combined frantic energy with eardrum-bursting sonic assault as administered by such as Van Halen, Bon Jovi, Guns N' Roses, Iron Maiden and Def Leppard. Punk outrage lived on more discernibly in death metal, an acute exaggeration of the more bloodstained preoccupations of Black Sabbath and Alice Cooper. Among its brand leaders are Megadeth, Carcass and Revulsion.

Certain death metal entertainers were not above the same old publicity stroke that everyone from Presley to the Sex Pistols had pulled—that they were nice lads when you got to know them. Pacifist and vegetarian Carcass, for example, consisted of two medical students and guitarist Bill Steer who was almost apologetic with his "I'm intrigued by mass murderers and that, but I think people take all the gory lyrics with a pinch of salt".

LONG LIVE ROCK?

Live Aid and Nostalgia

Frankie Goes To Hollywood. 'Relax' and 'Two Tribes' were No.1 and 2 in the UK charts for weeks in 1984.

FROM THE STARTING LINE OF 1971'S *CONCERTS FOR BANGLADESH*, ROCK CRANKED INTO TOP GEAR WHILE HURTLING ALONG THE ROAD TO RESPECTABILITY AFTER 1985'S *LIVE AID* EARNED THE BOOMTOWN RATS' BOB GELDOF A KNIGHTHOOD. FURTHER BIG-NAME ALTRUISM INCLUDED SMALLER CONCERTS FOR RESEARCH INTO VARIOUS AILMENTS, AND *OMNES FORTISSIMO* CHARITY 45S.

In the recessive years after punk, money could still be conned out of government aid to form a group, even if, in the same defeated climate, record companies were no longer chucking blank cheques about—except on dead certs like Dire Straits, Genesis and Stock-Aitken-Waterman creations by such as Rick Astley, Bananarama, Samantha Fox and Kylie Minogue. In northern England, three cities—Sheffield (home of the Human League, ABC, Clock DVA and Heaven 17), good old Liverpool (Frankie Goes To Hollywood, the Christians, Orchestral Manoeuvres In The Dark) and Manchester (New Order, the Smiths, Happy Mondays, the Stone Roses)—all had periods of being where it's at, and Donegal in Eire cradled Clannad and Enya, chart exemplars of ethereal New Age music.

New Tradition, a late development in country rock, encompassed the differing aptitudes of the Judds, k. d. lang, Randy Travis, Dwight Yoakam, Sweethearts Of The Rodeo and, most spectacularly, Garth Brooks, who were forsaking much of C&W's rhinestoned tackiness for a leaner, more abandoned approach. The USA also injected the most progressive serum into rock with the varying talents of the B52s, Laurie Anderson and the Kronos Quartet, while the UK did likewise with mainstream acts such as Bros, Wham!, Kim Wilde (daughter of Marty) and Duran Duran.

Though a case might be argued for Dublin's U2, geography and style did not polarize to any significant degree other incoming sounds such as the chameleon-like Dexy's Midnight Runners, the modern glam of Culture Club, Level 42 and Bryan Adams, whose workmanlike 'Everything I Do' was the longest-reigning UK Number 1.

In an age of consumption over creativity, just recording a single and all its different mixes was the least of your worries. What about the TV commercial to go with it? The half-page advertisement in a national tabloid? For the video, do you project the artist in a dramatic situation or in a straightforward synchronization with a musical performance? Yet, no matter how it was tarted up—12-inch megamix on polka-dot vinyl or whatever—the pop single had become a loss leader, an incentive for grown-ups to buy an album, hopefully on compact disc. Teenagers, you see, were no longer the market's most vital target group, having been outmanoeuvred by their Swinging Sixties parents and young marrieds who had sated their appetites for novelty. As in the pre-rock 'n' roll era, the young had to put up with pretty much the same music that their parents liked.

Rock's history as much as its present had been seized upon as an avenue for selling records. All it took, it seemed, was for a swarthy youth to take off his jeans in a launderette for a TV commercial, and Britain in the mid-Eighties was awash with nostalgia for the Sixties. At one stage, every fourth record in the UK Top 40 was either a reissue or a revival of an old chestnut. Resulting directly from snippet coverage in advertisements and movies were high chart placings for old discs by Ben E. King, Percy Sledge, the Hollies, the Steve Miller Band, Nina Simone, the Righteous Brothers and, from even further back, Eddie Cochran—all as out of step with the strident march of hip-hop, rap, acid house *et al*, as Viking long-ships docking in a hovercraft terminal.

In the States, jumping out of albums would be an artist's disposable revamp of an oldie, say, Cheap Trick's ham-fisted 'Don't Be Cruel' and Michael Bolton's Top 40 cover of Otis Redding's 'Dock Of The

Former soap-opera actress Kylie Minogue plugs her latest hit.

Bay'. In 1982, Van Halen touched Number 12 with Roy Orbison's 'Oh! Pretty Woman'; which the year before had resounded in the UK Top 10 as part of Tight Fit's 'Back To The Sixties' medley. Doing good business too were stylized musical plays like *Elvis* and *Beatlemania,* and imitation acts that included numberless Elvis and Beatles clones and, more recently, Bjorn Again (Abba) and the Scottish Sex Pistols.

Other performers were content simply to eulogize this or that old hero while buttressing their positions

U2 began as a Dublin punk group and evolved into Eighties stadium stars.

with a plausible influence. The six-tieth birthdays of Fats Domino and Chuck Berry were celebrated before television cameras in back-slapping fashion—though Joe Public might have preferred more typical recitals, unencumbered by the illustrious and more youthful friends who were giving the rock 'n' rollers a contemporary seal of approval to an almost palpable wave of goodwill.

Phil Lynott's 'King's Call'—about Elvis—and Psychic TV's 'Godstar'—on drowned Rolling Stone Brian Jones—will do as examples from what was a high summer of tribute discs. Moreover, two 45s by the Art Of Noise were collaborations with, respectively, Duane Eddy and Tom Jones. U2 cottoned on to blues sexagenarian B. B. King whose fretboard *obligatos* would tear at 1989's 'When Love Comes To Town', and the Kinks had been a source of hits for many groups including the Jam, the Pretenders and the Fall. Saddest of all was *Sgt. Pepper Knew My Father,* a charity LP

on which Wet Wet Wet, Billy Bragg and other new acts stood in for the Lonely Hearts Club Band for a remake of the Beatles' most famous record.

For all their wrinkles, galloping alopecia and belts at the last hole, it was now not out of the question for stars no longer young to re-enter the hit parade with their latest releases, aided by soft-focus publicity shots, and at a pace which often involved vanishing into the studio for years on end. Polished and pleasant, such albums were never expected to be astounding.

With six Grammy nominations for his hi-tech *Back In The High Life* album, diffident former Traffic man Steve Winwood was on the boards again for a trans-continental tour—as were Bob Dylan, Paul McCartney, the Rolling Stones, Leonard Cohen, the Who and Paul Simon. From the Stones packing out Madison Square Garden to Bobby Vee on the chicken-in-a-basket trail, it seemed

Enya, commercial apogee of New Age music, sprang from the same Irish family that produced Clannad.

that all acts still intact from as far back as the Fifties had somehow become archetypal units of their own, spanning, with different emphases, every familiar avenue of their professional careers—all the big hits, every bandwagon jumped, every change of image. With repackaging factories in full production by then, it made as much sense to plug recordings 30 years old as well as the most recent album that ticket-holders may or may not have heard.

ABC

From Yorkshire, this shiny-suited combo's début single, 'Tears Are Not Enough', sent them into the national Top 20 by late 1981. Fashionable producer Trevor Horn undertook the technological donkey-work of the 'Poison Arrow' and 'The Look Of Love' follow-ups which got them higher still. Both were tasters from *The Lexicon Of Love* which, in July 1982, crashed straight in at the top of the album chart. However, halting at Number 18, 1983's 'That Was Then But This Is Now', was a true comedown by previous standards, and after the second LP, self-produced *Beauty Stab*, had to be completed with backing musicians from Roxy Music, ABC weren't much of a group any more.

Singer Martin Fry and guitarist Mark White, the only original members left, enrolled new personnel for looks rather than musicianship, and remodelled themselves initially with biker apparel and a less lush sound to score a US hit with 1985's 'Be Near Me'. No time was worse for Fry to develop cancer but, on his recovery, ABC shrank to a fixed duo of him and White to chalk up a well-received 1987 album, *Alphabet City* and another hit single, 'When Smokey (Robinson) Sings'. Keeping FM radio in focus, they continued to enjoy further modest chart strikes.

ACE

Paul Carrack (vocals, keyboards) and Terence Comer (bass)—veterans of Warm Dust, a northern "progressive" outfit—joined Alan King (guitar)—formerly of Mod combo the Action—and Londoners Philip Harris (guitar) and Steven Witherington (drums) to work the pub-rock circuit in 1972. This beery schedule lasted two years during which time Francis Byrne from Bees Make Honey took over on drums. From a début album, *Five-A-Side*, 1974's self-composed 'How Long' (revived in 1982 by Rod Stewart) reached the UK Top 20 before an astonishing rise to the top of the US Hot 100.

Initially bewildered by their unexpected global fame, Ace's livelihood came to hinge on taking North America for every cent they could get. After the exit of Harris, the group emigrated in 1976 to California where Carrack's fondness for country-rock and Yankee slang in his lyrics contributed to the increased Americanization of Ace, as did the hiring of Los Angeles session musicians for 1977's slick *No Strings* album.

When Ace disbanded soon afterwards, Paul's tenacity in pursuing an alien culture was rewarded with a modicum of US solo success in the late Eighties, which was repeated in microcosm in Britain with minor hits 'When You Walk In The Room' and 1989's 'Don't Shed A Tear'.

ADAM AND THE ANTS

An appearance in the 1978 genre movie *Jubilee* got this London punk combo off the runway. Though beset with inconvenient personnel changes and often undeserved rubbishings in the music press, they worked up a fanatical grass-roots following. However, their records sold poorly and, in 1979, the Ants left Adam for Annabella Lwin, a client of Malcolm McLaren. If irked, Adam Ant derived artistic benefit from the former Sex Pistols' manager who'd played him tapes of African drumming and

Adam And The Ants dominated the British charts in the early Eighties before Adam went solo and began a withdrawal from pop.

suggested a new look—a hybrid of swashbuckling pirate and Red Indian. These ideas were incorporated into Ant's new backing group—guitar, bass and two drummers—and the songs he wrote with Marco Pirroni for *Kings Of The Wild Frontier*, a 1980 album that included Ant's first Top 10 hits, 'Dog Eat Dog' and 'Antmusic'. Repromoted, the title track would top the charts after 1981's 'Stand And Deliver' precipitated the "Antmania" that embraced another Number 1 with 'Prince Charming', and Top 40 entries for reactivated discs by the old outfit. It was after he went solo in 1982 that Ant made inroads into the US Top 20 before a calculated withdrawal from pop competitiveness to focus more on an acting career.

BRYAN ADAMS

Thanks in part to its use in 1991 feature film, *Robin Hood: Prince Of Thieves*, '(Everything I Do) I Do For You'—written and sung by this ordinary-looking, bedenimmed Canadian—spent longer at Number 1 in Britain than any other single before or since. If he lacked singular public personality, Adams was blessed with a gritty, commanding voice, instinctive audience control and a competent rhythm guitar style developed after he capitalized on the domestic hits that Ian Lloyd and Prism, a US outfit, had had with songs he'd written with Jim Vallance.

Leading his own quintet, the Dudes Of Leisure, Adams cracked the US Hot 100 with two singles from 1983's *Cut Like A Knife* before 'Run To You' caught on overseas 2 years later—though 'Heaven', a US chart-topper, made less of an impression elsewhere, despite an appearance on *Live Aid*.

Bryan Adams's 'Everything I Do' lingered at Number 1 in Britain for a record 3 months.

However, in that same year, 'It's Only Love' (a duet with Tina Turner) and the *Reckless* album were his biggest UK strikes prior to 'Everything I Do', which was followed by another smash in 'Thought I'd Died And Gone To Heaven' from *Waking Up The Neighbours*. On many tracks—and in recent concerts—the heavy metal lacerations of his lead guitarist, Keith Scott, are almost as prominent as Adams's own performances.

THE ANIMALS

The group was formed in 1962 from veterans of diverse skiffle, trad, rock 'n' roll and R&B outfits around Tyneside. All their early singles made the Top 10—with the second, 'House Of The Rising Sun', topping lists on both sides of the Atlantic. By 1965, a *New Musical Express* popularity poll had them breathing down the necks of the Beatles and the Stones. Alan Price (keyboards) then left to enjoy a run of solo hits while the others—Eric Burdon (vocals), Hilton Valentine (guitar), Chas Chandler (bass) and John Steel (drums)—carried on with Dave Rowberry from the Mike Cotton Sound. It was business as usual for the Animals until they disbanded in 1966 after 'Don't Bring Me Down' fell from its UK high of Number 6.

Burdon was persuaded to front a New Animals who continued to rake in the loot—largely with smashes of psychedelic bent—until 1969.

The old line-up reassembled for periodic reunion bashes at Newcastle City Hall, and for two albums—1976's *Before We Were So Rudely Interrupted* and, more conspicuously, *Ark* in 1983 which they promoted—along with a reissued 'House Of The Rising Sun'—on a world tour.

BEACH BOYS

See separate entry in the Legends section.

THE BEATLES

See separate entry in the Legends section.

BEE GEES

Barry, Maurice and Robin Gibb were regulars on Australian television's *Bandstand* around 1960. Most of their early records were flops but 1966's 'Spicks And Specks' had been a domestic chart-topper when they left for London after recruiting guitarist Vince Melouney and drummer Colin Peterson. After much media build-up,

The Bee Gees shortly after the exit of Vince Melouney. The next to go was drummer Colin Peterson (striped tie).

sepulchral 'New York Mining Disaster 1941' made the British and US Top 20s. Later in 1967, they had a UK Number 1 with 'Massachusetts'—but after 'I've Gotta Get A Message To You' did the same, internal squabbles reduced the group briefly to only Barry and Maurice before Robin rejoined after a solo smash with 'Saved By The Bell'. Backed by session players, the brothers made the first of umpteen come-backs with 1971's 'How Can You Mend A Broken Heart', a US million-seller.

Another slack period precipitated a shift towards disco—though they kept their trademark warbling harmonies. This paid big enough dividends, especially with the *Saturday Night Fever* sound track and its singles, for the trio to coast through the next decade. Yet, just to show they still could, they knocked out another major hit, 'You Win Again', in 1987.

CHUCK BERRY

This grand old man of rock began composing in the late Forties when leading his own trio. In 1955, he left his native Missouri for Chicago where he recorded his first single, 'Maybelline', a national Top 10 smash. 'Roll Over Beethoven', 'Sweet Little Sixteen', 'Johnny B Goode' and other Fifties hits celebrated in song the pleasures available to US teenage consumers, and would remain the cornerstone of Berry's stage act.

In 1959, he served the first of two jail terms that would put temporary halts to his career. Nevertheless, this incarceration boosted his cult celebrity in Britain where he'd only been seen derisively "duckwalking" with a crotch-level guitar in the Newport Jazz Festival film documentary, *Jazz on A Summer's Day*.

With his songs prominent in the repertoires of almost all beat groups, including the Beatles and Rolling Stones, he resurfaced in the UK Top 10 in 1963. Royalties amassed by innumerable covers, his reputation as a showman, and million-selling windfalls like 1972's lyrically dubious 'My Ding-A-Ling' have sustained him ever since.

In 1986, an all-star band, rather than his usual erratic pick-up group, backed him during the public celebration of his sixtieth birthday. This was turned into a movie, *Hail! Hail! Rock 'N' Roll* to tie in with the publication of his autobiography.

DAVE BERRY

Through one of pop's many arbitrary isolations, this Sheffield, UK, vocalist found himself the sudden Presley of the Flatlands after 1965's 'This Strange Effect', a comparative flop at home, became Holland's biggest-selling disc ever, and four previously released Berry singles appeared simultaneously in the Dutch Top 20. While he was not so fêted in Britain, the charismatic Berry and his backing Cruisers had been one of the north-east's most popular R&B groups 3 years before reaching the Top 20 in 1963 with a cover of Chuck Berry's 'Memphis Tennessee'.

After a smaller hit with 'My Baby Left Me', he veered closer to mainstream pop with smashes that included the much-covered 'Crying Game' (with its apt and unprecedented use of a nascent "wah-wah" guitar effect) and 'Little Things', but he was more remarkable for a surreal stage act, executed with all the spooky deliberation of a dream's slow motion. After 'This

Dave Berry, the "Presley of the Flatlands".

Strange Effect', he concentrated on Europe, where he remained a huge concert attraction, while drifting towards the UK cabaret and nostalgia market. However, by another strange twist, he came to be much admired by punk rockers such as the Sex Pistols and Adam Ant, and a 1986 album, *Hostage To The Beat*, was something of a critical *cause célèbre*.

BLACK SABBATH

A 1968 residency in Hamburg's Star-Club, Germany, invested this Midlands outfit's "progressive" blues style with a bleak but atmospheric intensity. Donning Satanic fetishist adornments, they delivered self-composed pieces that reflected occult interests. Some items appeared on an eponymous début album that visited the UK Top 10, as did a single, 'Paranoid'. From the 1970 album of the same name stemmed the group's international success— particularly in the USA—which continued throughout the Seventies with further output of similar doom laden stamp, the principal points of which were guitarist Tony Iommi's blistering solos and singer Ozzy Osbourne's straining attack. Eventually discord in the studio with the punctilious guitarist caused Osbourne's exit in 1978 to lead the Blizzards Of Oz as a significant rival attraction.

His replacement was Ronnie James Dio, an American, as was Vincent Appice who superseded drummer Bill Ward the following year. A slightly

Black Sabbath: John "Ozzy" Osbourne (far left) had success in the Eighties as leader of the Blizzards of Oz.

more subtle outlook marked the albums that preceded more personnel changes and the group's apparent disbandment in 1983. However, the original line-up reunited for *Live Aid*. Later, a "Black Sabbath With Tony Iommi" issued three albums but, though all sold moderately, most fans preferred the old monster.

MARC BOLAN/T REX

Bolan's cautionary tale began during the Sixties when he embraced respective careers as a Mod Ace face, would-be English Bob Dylan, guitarist with psychedelic John's Children, and cult figure with the Tyrannosaurus Rex acoustic duo. Yet, however disparate his vocational threads, all make discernible sense when set within their decade as he jumped bandwagons ahead of most rivals, and impregnated each genre with an inbred originality that rode rough-shod over less attractive traits like his ruthlessness when seeking renown and a talkative conceit when he achieved it after modest chart entries with Tyrannosaurus Rex.

In 1971, he went fully electric as leader of T Rex, the four-piece medium of his glam-rock stardom with UK chart-toppers 'Hot Love', 'Get It On' (his biggest US hit), 'Telegram Sam', 'Metal Guru' and 1971's *Electric Warrior* album. His period at the top was short but he fed off it as best he could, mainly by rehashing old ideas and attempting a sustained come-back as a grand old man of punk. However, he was a children's television presenter when killed in a 1977 car crash. It took an ITV commercial years afterwards to bring T Rex back into the Top 10—for it was Marc's hard luck that his spectacular James Dean-type exit took place within weeks of two other big deaths (Presley and Bing Crosby).

☆ ☆ ☆

DAVID BOWIE

See separate entry in the Legends section.

THE BYRDS

Individually, Jim McGuinn (guitar, vocals), Gene Clark (vocals, percussion), Dave Crosby (vocals, guitar), Chris Hillman (bass, vocals) and Michael Clarke (drums) served early Sixties folk and C&W acts like the Chad Mitchell Trio, the Hillmen and the New Christy Minstrels before amalgamating in Los Angeles during 1964's "British invasion", from which they derived a lasting benefit by developing the melodic vocal

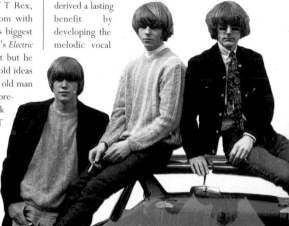

harmonies of the Searchers and, to a lesser degree, the Beatles, and, in McGuinn's purchase of a 12-string model, broadening the uniquely circular effect of fingerpicking two electric guitars.

From the Searchers too came the idea of merging Merseybeat and contemporary folk. Yet, though attributed to the Byrds, only McGuinn and session players were heard on their début 45, a million-selling version of Bob Dylan's 'Mr Tambourine Man'. Further hits came mostly from the group's own pens as they invested folk-rock, psychedelia and then C&W with a sound that was to become peculiar to themselves and their many copyists, notably Tom Petty And The Heartbreakers.

As the only original Byrd left by 1972, McGuinn—now with the new forename 'Roger'—disbanded the group. A few months later, however, the 1964 line-up convened to record what turned out to be a valedictory—and disappointing—eponymous album.

CANNED HEAT

They found each other during impromptu sessions in Los Angeles clubs. Balancing humour and scholarly application, much of this inspired good-time blues group's appeal lay in the solid musicianship of

The Byrds in 1965. By 1972, Roger McGuinn (sunglasses) was the only remaining original member.

ex-Mother Of Invention Henry Vestine (guitar), Larry Taylor (bass), and Frank Cook (drums), and the disparate natures of its front men: corpulent, jocular ex-supermarket chargehand Bob "Bear" Hite (vocals) and intense Alan "Blind Owl" Wilson (vocal, harmonica, guitar) with his master's degree.

After the unit's well-received performance at the Monterey International Pop Music Festival in 1967, a second album, *Boogie With Canned Heat,* and its attendant 'On The Road Again' hit established them as a world class act. 'Goin' Up The Country' and 1970's 'Let's Work Together' were also smashes, and the band became renowned for reliable entertainment at outdoor festivals from Woodstock downwards.

Though able to carry on in a recognizable form, the group proved incapable of major commercial or artistic recovery after Wilson's death in 1970 and a consequent flux of transient personnel that included Stan Webb from England's Chicken Shack. In 1981, Hite's fatal heart attack might have been an opportune moment for disbandment but, rallying once more, the droning rhythm synonymous with Canned Heat continued to underpin all the old crowd-pleasers as records became even less important than earnings on the road.

☆   ☆   ☆

CAPTAIN BEEFHEART

An acquired taste, this Californian was master and only practitioner of a self-originated art. Born Don Van Vliet, he was a painter and sculptor before the blast of his marvellous voice (sort of Howlin' Wolf meets Al Jolson) and unorthodox command of harmonica and saxophone were heard in local groups, including the Soots (with Frank Zappa) and, in 1964, the first of many backing Magic Bands. Ry Cooder passed through the ranks in 1967 when Beefheart's *Safe As Milk* album became the toast of hippy Europe. Next came the entirely self-composed *Strictly Personal* which he would disown after producer Bob Krasnow doctored it with phasing and other gimmicks to render it "modern" enough to sound dated by 1969 when the surreal *Trout Mask Replica* (produced by Zappa) crept into the UK album Top 30 after heavy Radio One plugging by presenter John Peel. This and its *Lick My Decals Off Baby* follow-up marked the Captain's commercial apogee, though later efforts tended to be less "difficult", even featuring the odd cover version. Though 1972's *The Spotlight Kid* took him into the US chart, it was the early offerings that came to be much-requested spins on punk turntables.

During the successively longer gaps between recording projects, he returned to painting and oversaw several exhibitions of his work, including a London opening in 1986, by which time he had all but withdrawn from the music business.

CHUBBY CHECKER

Born Ernest Evans, this vocalist from Philadelphia was known for his skill at impersonating other pop entertainers before a 1960 cover of Hank Ballard's R&B novelty, 'The Twist', set him up for life. This "most vulgar dance ever invented", reported a *Melody Maker* newshound, involved pretending to towel your back while grinding a cigarette butt with the foot. By the time, 'The Twist' went to Number 1 in the US for a second time in 1962, Checker had sold additional millions of discs based on the same format—'Let's Twist Again', 'Slow Twistin' *ad nauseam*— which, during countless television demonstrations, he propagated as a fun way to keep fit. Also in 1962, he teamed up with Bobby Rydell for 'Teach Me How To Twist'.

Next, he gave 'em 'The Hucklebuck'—revived in 1981 by Coast to Coast—'The Fly' and 'Limbo Rock' but 'The Twist' kept its palais popularity whether in Birmingham's Moat Twistacular or New York's swish Peppermint Lounge where middle-aged socialites mingled with beatniks until the craze died—but Checker kept plugging away with such as 1964's 'Do The Freddie' (a homage to Freddie and the Dreamers) and 'At The Discotheque' which had become a most desirable collector's item for Britain's "northern soul" DJs when a re-issued 'Let's Twist Again' hit the Top 10 in 1975. There it was again in 1988's US Top 20 as a rap by the Fat Boys with Chubby making a guest appearance, twisting for all eternity.

DAVE CLARK FIVE

Prior to the release of an instrumental single, 'Chaquita', in 1962, the departure of Mick Ryan (guitar), Stan Saxon (vocals, saxophone) and Chris Walls (bass) necessitated the transfer of guitarist Rick Huxley to bass, and Clark's recruitment of Lenny Davidson (guitar), Denis Payton (saxophone) and Mike Smith (vocals, keyboards). Over the next year, this London outfit switched its stylistic emphasis to vocals—a strategy that proved beneficial when a cover of the Contours' 'Do You Love Me' paved the way for a self-penned 1964 chart-topper, 'Glad All Over'. After the follow-up, 'Bits And Pieces', domestic chart entries were sporadic but, thanks partly to Clark's shrewd business acumen, the group racked up heftier achievements in the States as a foremost "British invasion" act.

While 'Catch Us If You Can' (from the Five's only major movie) was a hit on both sides of the Atlantic, output issued before disbandment in 1970 was characterized by much bandwagon-jumping and cover versions. Clark's main creative public activities since have been Seventies recordings with Smith as "Dave Clark And Friends", editing the Ready Steady Go archives, and 1987's *Time* musical. In 1978, the Five's *Twenty-Five Thumping Great Hits* climbed high in the British album chart, and a re-issued 'Glad All Over' entered the Top 40 in 1993 to tie in with the release of the Five's first CD, *Glad All Over Again*.

CLIMAX BLUES BAND

After global fame with R&B group Hipster Image proved elusive, Colin Cooper (vocals, guitar, saxophone) returned to his native Stafford where, from a pool of local musicians that included drummer John Cuffely (formerly with Emile Ford's Checkmates) and singing guitarist Peter Haycock, he formed the Gospel Truth, a sextet which he renamed the Climax Chicago Blues Band as a nod towards the British blues boom in the late Sixties. Over five albums they built up a following in Europe before shrinking in 1972 to a less cumbersome four-piece with Derek Holt (vocals, bass) and dropping 'Chicago' from their title. By then, they were concentrating on the US market where relentless touring was paying off with albums in the lower reaches of the charts.

However, with the higher placing of a New York concert offering, *FM Live*, which lingered on the Billboard chart for almost a year, they moved from being a reliable support act to headliners. Further albums compounded this breakthrough. A 1975 tour with Curved Air restored much lost popularity in Europe, and in 1976 they even made the UK Top 10 with 'Couldn't Get It Right' from the ITV-advertised *Gold-Plated*, which, of course, did even better in North America, a territory that would remain amenable to them until the advent of new wave. Pursuing a more middle-of-the-road route, the band remained a going concern with only Cooper left from the 1972 line-up.

JOE COCKER

After drumming with the Cavaliers, he became popular in his native Sheffield as figurehead of Vance Arnold And The Avengers, whose repertoire had veered from assembly-line pop to Cocker's blues and soul preferences by the time he reverted to his real name to front the Grease Band in 1966. A fleeting Top 50 entry with 1968's self-penned 'Marjorine' presaged a sweaty and chart-topping overhaul of the Beatles' 'With A Little Help From My Friends'.

This domestic triumph was, however, regarded by his investors as a dry-run for North America where he amassed and then lost a fortune via a lackadaisical regard for business following a successful performance at Woodstock and a disinclined tour as *de jure* leader of the oversubscribed Mad Dogs And Englishmen troupe of Hollywood "supersidemen", their hangers-on and what was left of the Grease Band. A come-back with a more manageable backing unit was marked by Joe's increasing intake of artificial stimulants and a resulting on-stage boorishness that, in the USA and Australasia at least, was lapped up by fans as the prerogative of glamour.

He remained virtually forgotten in Britain until 1983 when 'Up Where We Belong', a duet with Jennifer Warnes, penetrated the Top 10 after a spell at Number 1 in the States. Since then, he has settled down to regular tour-album-tour sandwiches as a rock treasure guaranteed well-paid work for as long as he can stand.

ALICE COOPER

In artistic debt to British beat, these Arizona musicians started as the Earwigs. Yet by the time they'd moved to Los Angeles in 1968, they'd become horror-rock executants Alice Cooper. Their first releases gave them a cult celebrity but, on moving to Detroit, they drew a following significant enough to place 'I'm Eighteen' in the national Top 40. The antithesis of post-Woodstock blandness, their glam rock from the charnel house stage presentation climaxed with the singer's "execution" for "felonies" committed during the act. However, the repellant allure generated diverted attention from the quality of albums such as *Killer, School's Out*—with its title track a UK Number 1—and 1974's *Muscle Of Love*. Many ideas were borrowed but, overall, the music amounted to a controlled, melodic vein of heavy rock underlining a macabre if witty lyricism.

When the ensemble disbanded in 1975, Cooper the vocalist employed session players for *Lace And Whisky* and other collections that preceded a spell in a clinic to treat his alcoholism—an experience that provided a theme for the 1978 come-back album, *From The Inside*. During the Eighties, his shows had period charm, and he wasn't beyond nearly topping both the UK album and singles charts in 1989 with *Trash* and 'Poison'.

Alice Cooper: glam-rock from the charnel house, featured on albums *Killer, School's Out* and *Muscle of Love*.

ELVIS COSTELLO

He was the most successful of a late Seventies crop of British composer-performers that included Wreckless Eric, Alan Clayson and John Otway. A series of inspired publicity stunts made his concerts seem like special events, and assisted the passage of his first album, 1977's *My Aim Is True*, and early singles into the UK charts. Backed by the Attractions, he touched a commercial zenith in 1979 with *Armed Forces* as his biggest US seller, and its 'Oliver's Army' spin-off at a domestic Number 2.

For such a prolific and "covered" songwriter, it was perhaps odd that he has since returned to the UK Top 10 only with items penned by others, i.e. Sam And Dave's 'I Can't Stand Up For Falling Down' (off 1980's *Get Happy*) and 'A Good Year For The Roses', a C&W moroseness from 1981's *Almost Blue*. Both were examples of Costello's frequent ventures into unexpected musical areas. Another is 1993's *The Juliet Letters* with the Brodsky Quartet, for which he reverted to his given name, Declan McManus. To the general public, however, a brighter feather in his cap had been a collaboration with Paul McCartney on pieces that appeared on their respective albums in the late Eighties.

THE CRAMPS

These New Yorkers' deepest musical roots lay in Southern rockabilly, though they traded not in the usual hepcat matters but the darker preoccupations implicated in titles like 'I Was A Teenage Werewolf', 'Zombie Dance' and 'Aloha From Hell'. They were tasteful in their selection of covers too, e.g. the Trashmen's 'Surfin' Bird', the Count Five's 'Psychotic Reaction'. They also risked

The Cramps: rockabilly from hell, as exemplified in titles like 'I Was A Teenage Werewolf' and 'Zombie Dance'.

doing without the obligatory bass guitar, relying on clangorous chord-slashing by Poison Ivy and Bryan Gregory and a basic off-beat from drummer Miriam Linna to back vocal extremist Lux Interior.

In 1976, they'd worked up a huge grass-roots following via regular appearances in the feted CBGB's club. However, a hand in 1977's *The Foreigner* film preceded the replacement of Linna with Nick Knox. After several singles and a début LP, *Songs The Lord Taught Us*, Gregory's exit in 1980 triggered the employment of a succession of second guitarists—mostly with lurid stage names. A surprisingly influential act, the Cramps are to be lauded for artistic consistency as, unbothered by slickness, they continue to deal in kitsch visuals, and the hair-raising impression that everything could fall to pieces at any moment.

CREEDENCE CLEARWATER REVIVAL

While John Fogerty (vocals, guitar), Tom Fogerty (guitar), Stuart Cook (bass) and Douglas Clifford (drums) didn't turn professional until 1967, this group harked back musically to the energy and many of the standard chord sequences of Fifties rock 'n' roll without actually looking the part, and with John Fogerty originals the backbone of their repertoire. Though Californian like the others, John's spiritual home seemed to be the Deep South, as exemplified in titles like 'Born On The Bayou' and 'Mardi Gras'.

After 1969's 'Proud Mary' all but topped the US chart, they reached a wider world too with the 12-bar 'Bad Moon Rising' at Number 1 in Britain and Australia, and similar performances elsewhere for the likes of 'Green River', 'Down On The Corner', 'Travelling Band', 'Up

Around The Bend' and attendant albums that met favour with heavy rock and mainstream pop fans alike. Whether appearing at Woodstock or on BBC children's television, it was all part of a day's work for Creedence, whose winning streak came to an end with the exit of the late Tom Fogerty in 1971, and Cook and Clifford's bigger say in artistic direction. After the unit disbanded in 1972, John Fogerty's solo hits included 'Rockin' All Over The World'—covered and adopted as a signature tune by Status Quo—and 1985's *Centrefield* album.

CROSBY, STILLS, NASH AND YOUNG

While on a US tour with the Hollies in 1968, Graham Nash had sown the seeds of a "supergroup" with ex-Byrd Dave Crosby and multi-instrumentalist Steve Stills. The new combine then rehearsed in London for an eponymous album notable for clever vocal harmonies, hippy lyricism and all the work of Stills—neo-acoustic backing tracks. Its single, Nash's 'Marrakesh Express', was a world-wide smash and, if the trio's warblings weren't to everyone's taste, he ended up a lot richer than if he'd stayed a Holly.

At Woodstock, the group's second booking, they were joined by Neil Young—a veteran of Buffalo Springfield like Stills—who stayed on for *Déjà Vu* on which needle-time was divided between items by the four composers and a version of Joni Mitchell's 'Woodstock'. With certain members going out with the same girl as well as Crosby's drug problems—which culminated in a jail sentence—and age-old tensions between Stills and Young building up, the unit split in 1972 to devote themselves mostly to solo careers, of which Young's was the most commercially successful. However, various combinations of the four teamed up over subsequent years for short-lived record and stage projects, and all reunited for *Live Aid* and 1988's *American Dream* album.

DEEP PURPLE

With individual pedigrees stretching back before Merseybeat, Deep Purple's first album, 1968's *Shades Of Deep Purple* (and its US hit single, 'Hush') gave few clues of what they were to become. After two more LP releases in the same vein, Rod Evans (vocals) and Nick Simper (bass) were replaced by Ian Gillan and Roger Glover.

Largely the work of Jon Lord (keyboards), 1970's *Concerto For Group And Orchestra*, an in-concert amalgam with the Royal Philharmonic, was notable for its Wagnerian unison riffs. It also showed a band in transition from mainstream pop to the heavy metal style blueprinted on *Deep Purple In Rock* and developed over subsequent early Seventies albums whose sleeves chronicled the personnel changes that preceded disbandment in 1976.

Of consequent splinter acts, the most popular were guitarist Ritchie Blackmore's Rainbow, and new vocalist David Coverdale's Whitesnake, which consisted mostly of ex-members when the 1970 line-up reformed in 1984 for a remunerative world tour and three albums before Gillan was superseded by Joe Lynn in 1990. By then, admirers of the Deep Purple of yore were more inclined to listen to Whitesnake as upholders of this tradition than anything Blackmore, Lord *et al* had to offer.

DEF LEPPARD

In 1977, Sheffield schoolboys drummer Tony Kenning, bassist Rick Savage and guitarist Pete Willis formed Atomic Mass, tight-trousered heavy metallurgists, who became Def Leppard with the addition of guitarist Steve Clarke and vocalist Joe Elliott. The new outfit suffered an immediate setback with the resignation of Kenning, necessitating the procurement of a series of transient drummers until the enlistment of Rick Allen in 1979. In the meantime, Elliott's father financed the launching of the group's own record label. An EP, 'Getcha Rocks Off', from this source was instrumental in the procurement of a long-term contract with Phonogram who may have visualized Def Leppard as a new Black Sabbath.

'Wasted', 'Hello America' and other minor UK hits set the juggernaut in quivering motion. From a début album, *On Through The Night*, stemmed the unit's US breakthrough, which was to culminate with 1987's *Hysteria,* the biggest selling US album by a British band and the restorer of much lost popularity at home.

However, for all their commercial achievements and their abstention from the usual rock 'n' roll vices, Def Leppard had more than their fair share of tragedy, notably in the 1984 car crash that left Allen with one arm and Clarke's sudden death in 1991.

Def Leppard, pride of Sheffield.

DIRE STRAITS

With homely ex-teacher Mark Knopfler (vocals, guitar) their main asset, and peddling adult "contemporary" rock at the height of punk, this London unit's name seemed apt until they were confronted with the enviable puzzle of being a world famous act with little big time experience after an eponymous début album and its 'Sultans Of Swing' 45 each shot into the respective US Top 5s. After a brief slackening of impetus, their third album, *Love Over Gold,* and those that followed went to Number 1 in the States with variable chart performances elsewhere. Each was dominated by Mark's songwriting, detached vocal style, production ideas and terse fretboard dexterity. Where appropriate, these skills gilded the works of Bob Dylan, Tina Turner—for whom he composed the hit single 'Private Dancer'—Bryan Ferry and others when he inaugurated a career separate from the group. This also embraced film sound tracks and the formation in 1989 of the Notting Hillbillies, a country-rock ensemble. Though Dire Straits had already endured the departures of drummer Pick Withers and Knopfler's guitarist brother David, Mark's extramural ventures have not been indicative of a more damaging schism in the ranks.

Lonnie Donegan, who bossed skiffle during its 1957 prime.

LONNIE DONEGAN

"The King of Skiffle" had drummed in a British army jazz band before plucking banjo for Ken Colyer and then Chris Barber. As a change from the usual trad jazz toot-tooting, both bandleaders permitted him to sing one or two blues-flavoured American folk tunes to the accompaniment of washboard, double bass and his own guitar strumming. From a 1954 Barber album, Lonnie's 'Rock Island Line' was released as a 45 to enter both the UK and US Top 10s.

Fronting his own skiffle group, Donegan's driving whine and vibrant personality lacquered further adaptations of similar North American material that, if failing to further his cause in the land from whence it came, kept him in domestic smashes, even after he offended purists by tilting for wider acceptance with singalongs from the Golden Days of Empire, such as 1960's chart-topping 'My Old Man's A Dustman'.

When the hits petered out around 1962, he was in a favourable negotiating position for personal appearances in cabaret and variety, with occasional windfalls from compilation albums and composing royalties for such as Tom Jones's 1967 cover of his 'I'll Never Fall In Love Again'. In 1978, he remade some of his Fifties favourites on *Putting On The Style*, an album produced by Adam Faith, though he had better luck with 1982's 'Spread A Little Happiness' when only a rival version by Sting prevented a return to the British singles chart.

THE DOORS

Singer Jim Morrison has been the posthumous subject of both a best-selling biography and a cinema film. Both fuel the myth that he *was* the Doors. While his ritualized cavortings on the boards brought the Los Angeles group much publicity—and notoriety—their recorded compositions were mostly either team efforts or by personnel other than Morrison, a poet whose lines were, nevertheless, the lyrical base of many numbers, such as 1967's 'Light My Fire', the US Number 1 that created demand for its album, *The Doors*, and the *Strange Days* follow-up. Further high placings in both the singles and album lists peaked in 1968 with chart-topping 'Hello I Love You'—which plagiarized a Kinks riff—and *Waiting For The Sun*. The turning of the tide may be dated from a 1969 concert in Miami where Morrison was alleged to have exposed himself. During a long wait for the "guilty" verdict with its resulting custodial sentence and appeal, he exiled himself to Paris where he passed away in 1971. His long shadow proved such a hindrance that the Doors broke up a year later, reuniting only to provide backing on *An American Prayer*, a 1978 album of Morrison reciting his deathless verse.

BOB DYLAN

See separate entry in the Legends section.

THE EAGLES

This outfit was formed in California largely from ex-backing musicians to the likes of Ricky Nelson, Bob Seger and Linda Ronstadt. They and singing composer Jackson Browne became hip Asylum Records' flagship acts after 1972's *Eagles* spawned three US hit 45s—the first, 'Take It Easy', co-written by Browne—all in popular country-rock vein. More of the same on 1973's thematic *Desperado* and *On The Border* led swiftly to years of national chart-toppers in both the album and singles lists, and more qualified strikes overseas where 1977's 'Hotel California' was the only 45 to reach Britain's Top 10.

By then, singing guitarist Bernard Leadon had been superseded by New Yorker Joe Walsh who put a promising solo career on hold for the three Eagles albums that preceded an amicable disbandment in 1981. These included *The Long Run*, on which Randy Meisner (bass, vocals) was replaced by Timothy B. Schmidt, and a 1980 in-concert finale. A re-formation has often been mooted, and fans might deem it significant that, as one of Ringo Starr's All Starr Band in 1989, Walsh chose to fill his lead vocal spot with the title track of *Desperado* rather than anything from his solo canon.

THE EASYBEATS

Formed in Sydney, Australia, in 1964, the Easybeats became too hot for the city to hold after a national Number 1 with 'She's So Fine'. After three more chart-toppers, it was a lengthy visit to Britain that brought the group to international attention with 1966's self-composed 'Friday On My Mind'. This attainment was dulled by the exit of drummer Gordon Fleet and a frustrating run of misses until the later Sixties when 'Hello How Are You' and 'St Louis' entered, respectively, the UK and US Top 40s. Despite a farewell trek round Australasia, the group's split in 1969 went so unnoticed elsewhere that the posthumous *Friends*, which entailed guitarists Harry Vanda and George Young only, was promoted as an Easybeats album. As a songwriting and production team, the pair were the brains behind Wright's solo come-back *Down Under* and *Flash And The Pan*, a studio-only entity that began an intermittent UK chart run in 1978 with 'And The Band Played On'. Much more spectacular was their financial and creative hand in the world-wide success of AC/DC, an outfit containing Young's two guitarist brothers.

GEORGIE FAME

Until 1962, Fame vacillated between stints as an uncomfortable English "answer" to Jerry Lee Lewis and as a mainstay of all-purpose backing combos on "scream circuit" package tours. However, changing from piano to organ, he came to front the Blue Flames who were popular in London's Mod clubland, where he taped *Live At The Flamingo*, the LP that heralded 1964's million-selling 'Yeah Yeah' and a chart run that included two more UK Number 1s in the self-composed 'Get Away' and—also a US Top 10 entry—1967's 'Ballad Of Bonnie And Clyde'. Also aimed at mainstream pop was a later merger with ex-Animal Alan Price, but Fame should be recognized too for excursions into jazz on albums like 1966's *Sound Venture* on which he was aided by such genre dignitaries as Tubby Hayes, Harry South and Stan Tracey.

The next year, a nervous Georgie sang with the Count Basie Orchestra at the Royal Albert Hall. In 1983, he'd be less intimidated by Annie Ross with whom he recorded a Hoagy Carmichael tribute album. Though there have been no more hits since 1971's 'Rosetta' (with Price), Fame is now financially secure not to need any, even if he is sometimes spotted in UK TV commercials and he continues to release pop albums like 1980's all-reggae *Closing The Gap*. In the Nineties, he was most often seen as leader of Van Morrison's accompanying ensemble.

BRYAN FERRY/
ROXY MUSIC

A former student of British pop-art pioneer Richard Hamilton, Bryan Ferry (vocals, keyboards) applied this received wisdom to rock on forming Roxy Music in 1971 with Phil Manzanera (guitar), Brian Eno (electronic effects), Andy Mackay (woodwinds), Graham Simpson (bass) and Paul Thompson (drums). After rehearsals and exploratory bookings, the group's first major engagement, at a pop festival in Lincoln, precipitated 5 fat years of UK hits, beginning with an eponymous début album—which elicited an immediate cover of its 'Sea Breezes' by Mike McGear—and a Top 10 single, 'Virginia Plain'. After 'Pyjamarama' and a second LP, *For Your Pleasure*, showed no relaxing of impetus, Ferry chanced a parallel solo career with an emphasis on non-originals.

With the success of these comparable to that of his work with the group, and the departure of the unconventionally gifted Eno, Roxy Music had become merely Ferry's backing outfit by the time it "devolved" in 1977 after scoring a modest US Hot 100 placing with 'Love Is The Drug'.

With Bryan's solo record sales depending almost entirely on commercial suitability, the band was reconstituted for an erratic four years before Ferry went off on his own, having so consolidated his fortunes that flop records could be shrugged off as life's loose change.

FLEETWOOD MAC

Guitarist Peter Green had been the star of John Mayall's Bluesbreakers in which Mick Fleetwood (drums) and John McVie (bass) had toiled less visibly. On leaving Mayall in 1967, the three became "Peter Green's Fleetwood Mac" after enlisting Jeremy Spencer, an Elmore James-style slide guitarist. Later, a third guitarist, Danny Kirwan, was added. The group began moving away from its blues core with 'Albatross', 'Oh Well' and other hit singles penned by Green.

Green's exit—and that of Spencer—in 1970 brought the outfit to its knees, despite the recruitment of McVie's personable wife Christine Perfect (ex-Chicken Shack) as singing pianist. More upheavals preceded the most commercially successful but volatile line-up—based in California by 1974—of the McVies, Fleetwood and US duo Stevie Nicks (vocals) and Lindsey Buckingham (guitar, vocals). With Buckingham, Nicks and Perfect writing the songs, personal tensions (such as John and Christine's divorce) lent pungency to huge-selling albums like *Rumours*, *Mirage* and 1987's *Tango In The Night*. By 1990's *Behind The Mask*, the plot had so thickened that Buckingham had quit (replaced by guitarist-vocalists Billy Burnette and Rick Vito), and Nicks and Perfect were considering doing so.

FOCUS

Thijs van Leer (keyboards, flute, vocals), Martin Dresden (bass) and Hans Cleuver (drums) began as hired accompanists to various vocalists and in a production of the *Hair* musical in their native Holland until the catalytic recruitment of guitarist Jan Akkerman. With a rather gimmicky "progressive" set that included rock adaptations of Rodrigo and Bartok, the outfit became popular in continental Europe before their second album, 1972's *Moving Waves*, almost topped the UK chart.

Of the original line-up, only Akkerman and van Leer remained on *Focus III*—and the singles 'Hocus Focus' and 'Sylvia' which visited Britain's Top 20 in 1973. After making more modest headway in North America, they marked time with an in-concert album.

Further mid-Seventies collections developed old ideas and, in 1975, Akkerman left, having recorded several solo efforts during his tenure with the band, as had van Leer who chose to lead a new Focus, whose output would embrace an album collaboration with P. J. Proby before disbandment in 1978.

Van Leer and Akkerman reunited in 1985 to supervise a Focus come-back album that made few ripples beyond the Flatlands and, 5 years later, the 1972 personnel regrouped for a one-off performance on a Dutch television special.

FREE/BAD COMPANY

Protégés of Alexis Korner, Paul Rodgers (vocals), Paul Kossoff (guitar), Andy Fraser (bass) and Simon Kirke (drums) gained enough support in British and European colleges in the late Sixties for their first two blues-derived albums to be worthwhile exercises financially. From sessions for a third, *Fire And Water*, emerged the self-composed 'All Right Now', which, sturdy if unoriginal, entered the Top 5 on both sides of the Atlantic, provoking one music journal to cite Free as "the new Stones". Though they never quite became that, they had more smashes both before and after breaking up in 1971 and regrouping briefly a year later.

With Boz Burrell (bass) from King Crimson and Mick Ralphs, Mott the Hoople's ex-guitarist, Kirke and Rodgers then formed Bad Company, a "supergroup" of sorts. Aimed at North America, an eponymous début LP topped the US list in 1974. Attended by spin-off smashes on 45 and coast-to-coast stadium tours, further musically unambitious but punchy offerings—notably *Straight Shooter* and 1979's valedictory *Desolation Angels*—were almost as lucrative. In 1986, a new Bad Company, with Brian Howe replacing Rodgers, hit the road—and the US charts—again as if the years since the previous incarnation had been mere weeks.

Jan Akkerman of Focus had 5 years' classical guitar training at Amsterdam Music Lyceum.

GENESIS

Peter Gabriel (vocals), Anthony Phillips (guitar), Tony Banks (keyboards), Mike Rutherford (bass) and Chris Stewart (drums) were a product of a top UK private school, and it was one of its old boys, pop star Jonathan King, who procured them a recording contract in 1969. Grass-roots support snowballed over two albums and a full calendar of mostly college bookings—but it wasn't for Phillips and Stewart who were replaced by Steve Hackett and, eventually, former child actor Phil Collins.

They broke into the UK charts with a fourth album, 1972's *Foxtrot*, which defined the dramatic "progressive" style that was to bring them to North America's attention with *The Lamb Lies Down On Broadway* in 1974, when Gabriel left to go solo. His slightly plummy vocals and startling stage outfits had become so integral to the band's character that many assumed they were finished. However, with the enlistment of drummer Bill Bruford (ex-Yes), Collins took over as singer, and the unit's commercial graph continued its upward turn, even through further personnel upheavals, lengthy sabbaticals, and the surprising success of Collins' solo records and film career in the Eighties.

The next decade showed no waning of Genesis' popularity with albums like 1992's *We Can't Dance* selling their usual millions.

GERRY AND THE PACEMAKERS

In 1963, this Merseyside outfit's first three singles—'How Do You Do It', 'I Like It' and 'You'll Never Walk Alone' all reached Number 1, a feat unmatched for 20 years. The self-composed 'I'm the One' almost made it four in a row but the going got rough after 'Don't Let The Sun Catch You Crying' seized up at Number 6, though it did establish the group—Gerry Marsden (vocals, guitar), Leslie Maguire (piano, saxophone, guitar), Les Chadwick (bass) and Freddie Marsden (drums)—in North America where previous releases—until repromoted—had fallen on stony ground.

An attempt to stay further decline was the four's starring roles in *Ferry Across The Mersey* with a title ballad that served as a requiem for Merseybeat's passing. With their very name a millstone round their necks, Gerry And The Pacemakers battled on until 1967 with distant chart victories in Australasia and the Far East.

After unfruitful bids for solo chartbusters, Gerry resurfaced as the "all-round entertainer" he'd always aspired to be, mainly on children's television and in West End musicals. Backed by new Pacemakers, he became a popular draw on nostalgia revues. To aid two Eighties disaster funds, he led all-star choirs through chart-topping remakes of 'You'll Never Walk Alone' and 'Ferry Across The Mersey'.

GARY GLITTER

Until his glam-rock supremacy in the Seventies, Paul Gadd had functioned as would-be English Elvis "Paul Raven", floor manager on ITV's *Ready Steady Go*, chief rabble-rouser with a soul band Forever in Germany, and bandwagon-jumper "Paul Munday" with a 1969 cover of the Beatles' 'Here Comes The Sun'. However unrewarding these experiences might have seemed at the time, they were to prove valuable when, as Gary Glitter, he came within an ace of topping both the British and US charts in 1972 with 'Rock And Roll Part 2'. This feat had come about as much through a liaison with producer Mike Leander as Gadd's new *nom de theatre* and trademark silvery stage costumes.

Of similar appeal, more big sellers, including a UK Number 1 hat-trick, established him as a glam-rock suzerain—its self-styled 'Leader Of The Gang'. Nevertheless, no further hits had been forthcoming in North America and, after a 1975 revival of the Rivingtons' 'Papa Oom Mow Mow' was a comparative miss at home, he "retired" briefly. After bankruptcy exacerbated by further chart flops, he managed a spectacular come-back in the Eighties as the kitsch king of the college circuit with a set containing nothing that hadn't been a smash for him, including his Top 10 return in 1984 with 'Another Rock And Roll Christmas'.

GRATEFUL DEAD

The most common name to trip off tongues discussing San Francisco "flower power" music, they'd been a part of an itinerant multi-media troupe, the Merry Band Of Pranksters, whose press releases promised, advisedly, a "drugless psychedelic experience".

From an R&B base, the Dead—Jerry Garcia (guitar, vocals), Bob Weir (guitar, vocals), Phil Lesh (vocals, bass), Ron McKernan (keyboards) and Bill Kreutzman (drums)—went in for much free-form instrumental meandering and nebulous augmentation on stage. This had to be reined in to stay within the limits of needle-time on studio albums like *Aoxomoxoa* and 1970's disciplined *Workingman's Dead*.

In 1972, McKernan's death coincided with an onslaught of critical derision for a grizzled hippy group that had become unfashionable well before Woodstock. Yet, buoyed by loyal "Deadheads" who'd pay to see them, regardless of passing fads, they approached the mid-Eighties as a massive concert draw, even a kind of national institution that could afford the Rex Foundation, a trust that—as well as more local causes—supports some of Britain's most experimental "serious" composers. With 1987's 'A Touch Of Grey' their first entry in the US Top 10, the Dead might be—as the title of a 1989 album states—*Built To Last* indeed.

Guns N' Roses' Axl Rose swings gently.

GUNS N' ROSES

Storming out of Los Angeles in the mid-Eighties, these rabble-rousers—Axl Rose (vocals), Tracii Guns (guitar), Izzy Stradlin (guitar), Michael McKagan (bass) and Rob Gardner (drums)—alienated even Swinging Sixties parents with their heavy metal-cum-punk racket and oafish "rock 'n' roll" behaviour that might have been connected to crass but effective marketing ploys. As such they became idols of would-be adolescent tearaways as the Rolling Stones had been around the time that most of Guns N' Roses were born. Too hot for LA to hold by 1986, the group were unable to play beyond its environs until homebodies Gardner and Guns were replaced by Saul "Slash" Hudson and Steven Adler.

A début album, *Appetite For Destruction*, gave a fair indication of future policy with a portrayal of mechanoid rape on a widely banned sleeve. The controversy helped its slow climb to Number 1 in the US; a coup carried out with much greater speed in the singles list with 'Sweet Child of Mine'.

Incessant world touring obliged them to buoy a second album, *GN'R Lies*, with previously issued tracks but no noticeable damage was done as, in hard financial terms, it was almost as big world-wide as *Appetite For Destruction*, and 1991's *Use Your Illusion*, though a double album, charged even more swiftly to the top.

JOHNNY HALLYDAY

Born Jean-Phillipe Smet, he is possibly the only French entertainer who, owing much to Elvis Presley, enjoyed anything like renown beyond domestic frontiers. Indeed, he sounded so like the King during a début radio broadcast in 1960 that he was hastened into the studio for an immediate single. Progress was, however, sluggish until late the following year when a bilingual version of Chubby Checker's 'Let's Twist Again' was a huge European smash.

Further US covers and various movie roles consolidated this breakthrough. The beat boom brought further lucrative but stylish bandwagon-jumping—a policy that was also applied to later trends. Rare appearances in English-speaking territories were well received, and an attendance figure of nearly 30,000 for a Hallyday concert in Latin America was not at all unusual. In the early Seventies, he was even the subject of a glowing feature in *Rolling Stone*.

His albums nearly always contained self-penned selections and, unlike most other Gallic rock stars, he adhered to the most up-to-date recording standards and album artwork as exemplified by 1975's *Flagrant Delit* taped mostly in Los Angeles with the cream of the city's "supersidemen". A couple of years later, he was in Nashville for an intriguing duet of 'If I Were A Carpenter' with Emmylou Harris.

GEORGE HARRISON

When a Beatle, he'd recorded two solo albums—the film sound track to *Wonderwall* and 1969's *Electronic Sounds*—but it was his progress as the more orthodox composer of such as 'Something' (as much a showbiz "standard" as 'Yesterday') that was among factors that led to the group's 1970 disbandment. He had, therefore, laid a solid foundation for a career as an ex-Beatle—which began well with a triple LP, *All Things Must Pass,* and its single, 'My Sweet Lord', each selling millions. As the leader of 1971's all-star *Concerts For Bangladesh,* he surfaced as the most respected and, seemingly, capable former Beatle.

His religious beliefs were refined on the self-produced *Living In The Material World* album but these were less pronounced on *Dark Horse*, promoted on a 1974 tour of North American so dogged by media criticism that he wasn't to undertake any like projects on the same scale.

Too mixed a reaction to his records coupled with a confidence-draining defeat when sued for plagiarism in 1976 dictated a gradual withdrawal from pop to concentrate on environmental issues and his successful Handmade Films company. In 1987, however, he returned to prominence in the charts with two singles from *Cloud Nine* and as founder member of the Traveling Wilburys "supergroup".

HEAVEN 17

On quitting the Human League in 1980, synthesizer players Ian Craig Marsh and Martyn Ware set up a creative production company, the British Electric Foundation, before teaming up with singer Glenn Gregory as Heaven 17 for a small beginning with the BBC-banned 'We Don't Need This Fascist Groove Thing' at Number 45. Moderate single hits were sufficient to hoist *Penthouse And Pavement* into the album Top 20, and 1983's 'Temptation'—also their US Hot 100 breakthrough—to one place short of the top. As a result, later discs like 'Come Live With Me'—another Top 5 smash—'Crushed By The Wheels Of Industry' and best-selling LP *The Luxury Gap* were guaranteed a fairer hearing.

Though a remixed 'Temptation' was to crack the UK Top 40 in 1992, hits had been thin on the ground after 1986's 'Trouble' stalled at Number 51. Yet, commanding much respect within the record industry, Marsh and Ware were in demand as producers after they'd framed Tina Turner's Top 10 come-back, 'Let's Stay Together'. Spreading itself more thinly in 1982, the British Electric Foundation's inspired *Music Of Quality And Distinction* compilation had been designed to please everybody with Gregory, Gary Glitter, Sandie Shaw and other hand-picked vocalists' attempts at numbers from the hit repertoires of others.

JIMI HENDRIX EXPERIENCE

Co-managed by ex-Animal Chas Chandler, Seattle-born singing guitarist Hendrix was brought in 1966 to London where the Experience—with Noel Redding (bass) and John Mitchell (drums)—was built round him. British Top 10 smashes with 'Hey Joe', 'Purple Haze' and 'The Wind Cries Mary' as well as the albums *Are You Experienced?* and *Axis: Bold As Love* set Hendrix and his group on the path to the global success that was sealed by a show-stealing performance at 1967's Monterey Pop Festival. It was showmanship as much as his innovative fretboard fireworks—and his accompanists' quick-witted responses—that was to make Hendrix a hit at Woodstock too after 1968's *Electric Ladyland* topped the US album chart.

A spell as leader of the all-American Band Of Gypsies with Billy Cox (bass) and Buddy Miles (drums) preceded a brief stage reunion with his English colleagues. With personnel from both outfits, he undertook some European dates in 1970 before his sudden death that September.

'Voodoo Chile' was lifted as an obvious single from *Electric Ladyland* and soared to a UK Number 1 within weeks. Though pundits had been dismissive of his latter-day output, there was a volte-face of favourable retrospection of the five albums officially issued during Jimi's lifetime—and many of the 300-odd with him as selling-point that have been released since.

The Jimi Hendrix Experience

HERMAN'S HERMITS

No one had achieved a qualified fame as a television soap-opera actor by 1964 when Mickie Most produced this Manchester outfit's first 45, 'I'm Into Something Good' (with help from the cream of London's session players). After this topped the domestic chart, it caught on in North America where little-boy-lost singer Peter "Herman" Noone could hardly fail at the apogee of the "British invasion". Indeed, "Hermania" plagued the continent throughout 1965 and 1966 as manifested by high Hot 100 climbs for such as 'Silhouettes', 'Mrs Brown You've Got A Lovely Daughter' and 'Listen People' before a predictable decline when new sensations, notably the Monkees, arrived. Turning back on the home market, Herman's Hermits managed a few more chart strikes before Noone went solo in 1971.

Most of his backing musicians made up a Herman's Hermits that was to find work on the nostalgia circuit. Sometimes they were joined by Noone who, after a UK Top 20 entry with David Bowie's 'Oh You Pretty Thing', tried light opera amongst other projects before an attempted return to rock in the early Eighties, fronting the Tremblers, though few were able to disassociate him from cuddlesome Herman.

THE HOLLIES

The career of Manchester's most acclaimed group—originally Allan Clarke (lead vocals), Graham Nash (vocals, rhythm guitar), Victor Farrell (lead guitar), Eric Haydock (bass) and Donald Rathbone (drums)—moved out of neutral in 1963 when Farrell and Rathbone were replaced, respectively, by Tony Hicks and Bobby Elliott from another local outfit, the Dolphins. The five's early hits—mostly from US sources—revealed the gradual development of the breathtaking vocal harmonies of Clarke, Hicks and Nash that were to serve them ever better when, under the pseudonym, "L. Ransford", the three began composing the group's A-sides. It was, however, a non-original, 1965's 'Look Through Any Window', that gave the Hollies a long-awaited Hot 100 début.

Internal discord led to the departure of Haydock and, more regrettably, songwriting pivot Nash (to the Crosby, Stills and Nash "supergroup"). Clarke too was to leave briefly for a couple of solo albums. Nevertheless, the smashes kept on coming, up to 1974's 'The Air That I Breathe'. After this slipped from Number 2 in Britain, there were only minor chart entries apart from a revival of the Supremes' 'Stop In The Name Of Love' that swept into the US Top 20 in 1983 and, via its use in an ITV commercial, the 20-year-old 'He Ain't Heavy (He's My Brother)' as a UK Number 1 in 1988.

BUDDY HOLLY

Profoundly awed by an Elvis Presley stage performance, this Texan singer and guitarist formed the Crickets—later, Buddy Holly And The Crickets—in 1956. After some unhappy sessions in Nashville, the outfit made more viable recordings in a New Mexico studio run by Norman Petty. Usually with help from this catalytic mentor and/or various Crickets, Holly wrote his own songs, and this ability plus the compact sound of two guitars, bass and drums on the group's only UK tour was one of the major elements that coalesced to produce the British beat boom. This 1958 visit was in the wake of a string of international hits that began with 1957's 'That'll Be The Day'.

In the aftershock of his death in an air crash in 1959, US obituarists tended to write Holly off as a has-been, especially as his latest 45, 'Heartbeat', had been a comparative flop. Nevertheless, the rush-released 'It Doesn't Matter Any More' was an enormous hit, resuscitating a flagging career. A subsequent schedule of reissues and previously unreleased tracks kept him in intermittent chart entries well into the Eighties, aided by a 1979 bio-pic as well as the annual "Buddy Holly Weeks" held in Britain since Paul McCartney's acquisition of Holly's publishing rights in the Seventies.

HUMAN LEAGUE

This futuristic Sheffield outfit's début 45, 1978's 'Being Boiled', was a highlight of recitals during which synthesizers kept pace with Phil Oakey's singing to a back projection of slides. Becoming noticed via an onslaught of publicity angles (e.g. Oakey's gimmick haircut), relentless touring and public praise from such as David Bowie, the group irritated the lowlier reaches of the UK charts with a mixture of originals and covers of numbers by the Righteous Brothers, Gary Glitter and Iggy Pop. When synthesizer players

By 1990, the Human League consisted of Phil Oakey (standing far right), the two girls and hired personnel.

Ian Craig Marsh and Martyn Ware left in 1980, a desperate Oakey and Adrian Wright (keyboards) roped in Jo Callis (guitar), Ian Burden (bass) and singers Joanne Catherall and Suzanne Sulley.

The new edition proved successful when, after 'The Sound Of The Crowd' ascended the Top 20, smash followed world-wide smash throughout the early Eighties. These included a repromoted 'Being Boiled' and the *Dare!* LP in the aftershock of a 1981 Number 1 single in both Britain and the USA with its boy-girl narrative 'Don't You Want Me'.

Hits became less frequent as the decade wore on, and the band had boiled down to Oakey and the girls plus hired personnel by 1992 when 'Don't You Want Me' was the subject of a Top 10 revival by the Farm.

JAN AND DEAN

In the late Fifties, Jan Berry and Dean Torrance were members of a Los Angeles high school group, the Barons, before Berry and Arnold Ginsberg recorded singles as Jan And Arnie—until Ginsberg's departure and Torrance's return from an obligatory spell in the US army.

Of Jan And Dean's early releases, only 1961's 'Heart and Soul' made major chart impact. Yet the vocal duo were well placed to cash in on the Californian surfing craze two years later. Co-written by Beach Boy Brian Wilson (who also

added a cruising falsetto) 'Surf City' was a US Number 1. Lesser hits included two paeans to drag-racing—1964's 'The Little Old Lady From Pasadena'—and 'Dead Man's Curve', a "death disc" that almost mirrored in fiction the 1966 car accident that left Berry severely paralysed and finished Jan And Dean's musical partnership for the next few years.

Though his bodily co-ordination and speech weren't what they were, Berry reunited with Torrance for the troubled 1973 come-back concert that was to be romanticized in the climax of the pair's *Dead Man's Curve* biopic of 1978. This exposure boosted interest in Jan And Dean appearances on nostalgia presentations, compilations of their hits, and a 1985 album of new material.

JETHRO TULL

Since the "British blues boom" in the late Sixties, this British outfit—originally Ian Anderson (vocals, flute, guitar), Mick Abrahams (guitar), Glenn Cornick (bass) and Clive Bunker (drums)—has retained an artistic individuality while absorbing many other musical idioms, even though the only constant element has been composer Ian Anderson. The image of his vagrant attire, matted hair and antics with the flute on UK TV's *Top Of The Pops* is not easily forgotten.

This exposure came after the group's third 45, 1969's 'Living In The Past', proved that as well as being a moderately popular album act since 1968's *This Was* début,

Tull were Top 10 singles merchants too. Before this break-through, Abrahams had been replaced by Martin Barre who was present on a second LP, *Stand Up*, which sold well in North America. Entries in the UK singles chart ceased—bar odd minor hits—by 1971 when *Aqualung*, the first Jethro Tull concept album, appeared. Such output was coalesced in the later Seventies less by lyrics than by style as exemplified by the folky album *Songs From The Wood*.

By the Eighties, Jethro Tull had become Anderson plus backing musicians whose high wages depend mostly upon US consumers' continued liking for 1987's Grammy-winning *Crest Of A Knave* and whatever other albums the financially secure Anderson chooses to record.

ELTON JOHN

He was pub pianist Reg Dwight before composing and singing 1965's 'Come Back Baby', the début 45 of Bluesology who were omnipresent as a backing band to US soul entertainers who visited Britain. When the group disbanded, Dwight renamed himself "Elton John" to begin a 10-year partnership with lyricist Bernie Taupin, initially as songsmiths for Dick James Music who also engaged John as a solo recording artist.

After 1970's *Elton John* spent a respectable 3 months in the album chart, he became a pop star proper with a Top 10 strike for 'Your Song'. Like much of his early Seventies output, this emitted the trendy drip-rock

romanticism that facilitated a North American break-through and a consequent series of seven consecutive US Number 1 albums.

By 1975's autobiographical *Captain Fantastic And The Brown Dirt Cowboy* a new Elton had emerged. A cross between Liberace and a male Edna Everage, he'd become considerably more animated on stage, having learnt a lot from soul revues with Bluesology. Though 1985's 'Nikita' showed he'd always be capable of chart-busting "beautiful sadness", he'd long rid himself of previous preciousness to enter middle life as one of the world's most popular acts, and a fully integrated mainstay and wanted party guest of "contemporary" rock's ruling class.

TOM JONES

Before a renaming in 1964 by manager Gordon Mills, he'd fronted the Senators as Tommy Scott, "The Twisting Vocalist from Pontypridd". However, the group faded away soon after their singer scented success with 1965's chart-topping 'It's Not Unusual' What *was* unusual was that he was not effeminate or subversive like a Jagger or Lennon who "couldn't sing" anyway. Instead, he was a robust hunk with a pile-driving but flexible vocal command and a steady consistency—"squareness", some would say. Indeed, 1966 was a lean year until 'Green

Jethro Tull's début 45, 'Sunshine Day', was erroneously attributed to "Jethro Toe". Far left, Ian Anderson plays flute.

Green Grass Of Home' restored him to Number 1. Further UK Top 20 entries stretched to the early Seventies, and the magnificence of his voice so smothered 'The Young New Mexican Puppeteer' and other piffle that he was second only to Joe Cocker in 1969's *Beat Instrumental* readers' poll. By then, he had found an apparent niche as a tuxedoed Las Vegas cabaret performer, but, just after his son Mark took over from the late Mills, Jones had a huge hit with 'The Boy From Nowhere' and a lesser one with a reissued 'It's Not Unusual'. Suddenly hip, he had another smash in 1990 with a version of Prince's 'Kiss', and was cool enough to star in a television documentary by Malcolm McLaren. In 1993, he revived the Beatles' 'All You Need Is Love' as a fund-raising single for a UK child abuse charity.

KINKS

After their third 45, 1964's 'You Really Got Me', earned them their first UK Number 1, this London outfit stuck to the same riff-based formula for several more smashes—bar the Eastern-flavoured 'See My Friends'. All were written by Ray Davies (vocals, guitar, keyboards) whose standing as a composer rose when he developed a more "English" style in the mid-Sixties. While the transitional *Face To Face*, 1968's *Village Green Preservation Society* and other albums of this era could not match the sales of earlier efforts, hits continued on the singles front with the likes of 'Sunny Afternoon', 'Waterloo Sunset' and

1970's 'Lola', as well a couple of solo offerings from Ray's lead guitarist brother Dave.

Personnel reshuffles included the resignation of Pete Quaife (bass), and the employment of auxiliary players for Ray Davies's ambitious "concept" albums and stage presentations of the Seventies. Without exception, neither these nor their spin-off singles made the charts. Fortune smiled again with the unexpected ascent of 1979's *Low Budget* into the *Billboard* album chart, and a fleeting return to the UK Top 20 4 years later with 'Come Dancing' but, even without these latter-day windfalls and the more recent departure of original drummer Mick Avory, the Kinks' stamp on rock is ingrained.

KRAFTWERK

With their state-of-the-art musical machinery effortlessly keeping pace with detached singing, this German outfit's records exuded a cold appeal so often found in Germanic rock. Though singing synthesizer players Ralf Hutter and Florian Schneider were the only mainstays, the group functioned as a quartet that at different times would include a violinist doubling on guitar, a flautist and additional synthesizer programmers. Their English-language records began creeping into the British and US charts after 1975's 'Autobahn' and an album of the same name each reached respective UK Top 20s. Further commercial progress was patchy until the Eighties when a minor hit with 'Pocket Calculator' preluded a "sleeper" Number 1 with 'The Model', a 3-year-old album track that had been pressed initially as the B-side of 1981's 'Computer Love'.

So passed the commercial apogee of German rock during which Kraftwerk undertook a world tour with an immobile, besuited stage presentation that nevertheless betrayed sufficient underlying humour to ensure that reviewers didn't understand how they were supposed to take it. Afterwards, the band found a level in the middle league of the rock hierarchy before a final chart entry with 1986's *Electric Café*.

BILLY J. KRAMER

William Howard Ashton served Liverpool's Billy Forde and the Phantoms before fronting the Coasters (not the US group) as "Billy Kramer". The group began thinking about turning professional after finding themselves two places behind the Beatles in *Merseybeat* magazine's 1963 popularity poll. However, recognized as the only one that mattered, only Billy was covered by a management agreement with Brian Epstein, who had the Coasters replaced by Manchester's more competent Dakotas and, at John Lennon's recommendation, split the new signing's stage name with a non-signifying initial. Lennon—and Paul McCartney— also supplied Billy J. Kramer with his first three UK hits, 'Do You Want To Know A Secret', chart-topping 'Bad To Me' and 'I'll Keep You Satisfied'.

Early in 1964 came 'Little Children', another UK Number 1—and his biggest US smash. A year later, how-ever, Billy's chart career ended with a cover of Burt Bacharach's 'Trains And Boats And Planes'. Keeping the wolf from the door with variety seasons, pantomime and as a compère on children's television, Kramer try-tried again with a patchwork of diverse styles on singles that included one by "William Howard Ashton". While his tenacity is to be admired, all his latter-day efforts pointed in the same direction: the Sixties nostalgia circuit.

Billy J. fronts the Dakotas—whose non-Liverpool origins were not stressed.

JOHN LENNON

While still a Beatle, his extramural projects included two volumes of verse, prose and cartoons, and bit-parts in television and cinema films. With performance artist Yoko Ono (later, the second Mrs Lennon), he realized a trilogy of controversial albums that were more documentary than recreational, as well as two hit singles—'Give Peace A Chance' and 'Instant Karma'—and an in-concert album with the *ad hoc* Plastic Ono Band. Some items were vehicles for the idiosyncratic support he lent to world peace and more precise causes.

His eponymous début album as an ex-Beatle was something of a public exorcism. Elements of this pervaded 1971's *Imagine* which also contained paeans of uxorious bent (e.g. 'Jealous Guy', 'Oh Yoko') and a title track that would emerge as Lennon's most memorable post-Beatle opus.

Resident in the States from 1972, he reverted to sloganeering protest on *Sometime In New York City* before spending a lengthy separation from his wife in Los Angeles where he tried to keep personal phantoms at bay with booze, drugs and grindstone albums, though 1974's *Walls And Bridges* included the US Number 1, 'Whatever Gets You Through The Night'.

Mastering his inner chaos, he returned to New York for five years of cheerful artistic lassitude before recording 1980's *Double Fantasy* (a joint effort with Yoko) a few months before he was shot dead by a "fan".

JERRY LEE LEWIS

Having married twice and begun training for the ministry before he was 16, "the Killer" balanced outrage and piety during a poor upbringing in Louisiana where he taught himself to play piano and sing in the unique fashion that got him through rough nights entertaining in local saloons, and gained him a contract with celebrated Sun Records in 1955.

His second single, 'Whole Lotta Shakin Goin' On', and attendant electrifying appearances on television catapulted him to national attention. The momentum was sustained with such seminal singles as 'Great Balls Of Fire' and 'High School Confidential' before a tour of Britain brought to light his bigamous third espousal to an under-aged cousin.

Though the scandal precipitated falling disc sales, he still scored occasionally in the charts with such as 'What I'd Say', a 1963 revival of Little Richard's 'Good Golly, Miss Molly', and, by the mid Sixties, he'd become a guaranteed crowd-puller once again. During this less prudish decade, publicity from Jerry Lee's brushes with the law, bouts of poor health brought on by over-indulgence and further marital ructions only gilded the legend. Though his rock 'n' roll classics would always be at the heart of his concert sets, as a recording artist, he managed to reinvent himself as a C&W star with such as 'What Made Milwaukee Famous', 'Boogie-Woogie Country Man' and 1986's 'Let My Fingers Do The Talking'.

LITTLE RICHARD

"The Georgia Peach" had his first hit in 1955 after an otherwise dull 1955 session spawned 'Tutti Frutti'. He remained a chart fixture for the next 3 years with such rock 'n' roll set works as 'Rip It Up', 'Long Tall Sally' and 1958's 'Good Golly Miss Molly', all dominated by Richard's vamping piano and declamatory vocal. Nevertheless, by the end of the Fifties, he had eschewed pop for the Church. While at theological college and a subsequent ministry, he released little but religious material for a few years. However, his 1962 gospel tour of the world had become a straight rock 'n' roll show by the time it reached Europe.

His influence was felt keenly during the British beat boom when singers like Paul McCartney or the Dave Clark Five's Mike Smith let rip, and Slade made a UK Top 20 début in 1971 with an adaptation of his 'Get Down With It' of 1966. Yet Richard himself generated sparse chart action after 1964's 'Bama Lama Bama Loo'. Since a foreseeable climbing on the nostalgia bandwagon, however, he has usually been received with much affection, and his ancient smashes have been kept before the public via such as the airing of 'Tutti Frutti' over the credits of a 1987 BBC television series about an old-fashioned rock 'n' roll group.

THE MAMAS AND THE PAPAS

The vigorous and contrapuntal chorale of Michelle Gilliam, Cass Elliott, John Phillips and Denny Doherty evolved in 1964 during sing-songs held when its future members were holidaying together in the Virgin Islands. They had all been part of the folk and fringe theatre scene in New York, and it made sense to team up to try their luck in Los Angeles where Phillips had useful connections in the West Coast record business.

Accompanied by session musicians, the outfit's first two singles, 'California Dreamin'' and 'Monday Monday' were followed by further international hits, mostly penned by Phillips who'd been on the steering committee of 1967's Monterey International Pop Music Festival where the group's performance—seen too in a spin-off movie—enhanced their standing as darlings of would-be hippies throughout the globe.

The break up of Phillips and Gilliam's marriage, the former's worsening drug addiction and a vexing run of comparative flops led to disbandment in 1968 but all ex-personnel remained in the entertainment industry. However, only Elliott sustained any measure of chart success, principally in Britain where she died in 1974.

Twelve years later, Doherty and a healthier Phillips—with two new female vocalists—took a Mamas And Papas on the first of many tours on the nostalgia circuit.

MANFRED MANN

This multifaceted UK ensemble—Paul Jones (vocals, harmonica), Mike Vickers (guitar, woodwinds), Manfred Mann (keyboards), Dave Richmond (bass) and Mike Hugg (drums)—first reached the Top 20 with 1964's '54321'. After 'Hubble Bubble' did likewise, Tom McGuinness superseded Dave Richmond, and, despite other personnel changes over the next few years, there was no let-up of chart entries until a flop with 'So Long Dad' in 1968. Some of the group's most enduring tracks were penned by Bob Dylan, who considered Manfred Mann the most proficient exponents of his work.

Allowing McGuinness to switch to guitar, bass player Jack Bruce passed through the ranks in 1966, as did a horn section. The most potentially injurious departure was that of singer Paul Jones that same year, but Mike d'Abo (from A Band Of Angels) proved a formidable successor before the outfit broke up in 1969. All former members were to achieve further success in the music industry— most conspicuously McGuinness,

whose McGuinness-Flint unit had two fast hits in the early Seventies, and Manfred Mann's Earth Band with a longer chart run later in the decade. In 1979, Jones and other ex-Mann men formed the much-loved Blues Band, who were still in business in 1992 when the 1965 line-up minus Mann but plus d'Abo (doubling on keyboards) undertook a UK tour as the Manfreds.

BOB MARLEY

This principal catalyst in bringing reggae to post-Woodstock rock had been a recording artist in his native Jamaica since 1962. His first efforts—and smart, short-haired image—were directed at a mainstream pop forum. Yet Marley and his backing Wailers' escape from parochial orbits began when they adopted a more indigenous sound and look on becoming dreadlocked Rastafarians—a ghetto religious sect—a conversion annotated in Marley lyrics of the later Sixties when every one of his singles was an automatic chart-topper in the West Indies.

Initially, success beyond the Caribbean was by proxy when Johnny Nash's cover of Marley's 'Stir It Up' reached the UK Top 10 in 1972. The following year, the Marley group's *Catch A Fire* and *Burnin'* (containing the much-covered 'I Shot The Sheriff') brought them an international groundswell of support in Europe and North America. Next, *Natty Dread* entered the UK album list, with 1976's *Rastaman Vibration* likewise doing the trick in the States. Though later Marley releases encompassed a swing towards a more consciously commercial approach, 1980's valedictory *Uprising*—issued a year before his death—gave indications that future output might have been channelled back to the black market for which it was always intended.

Manfred Mann in 1968. Clockwise from back left: Mann, McGuinness, Hugg, Voorman, d'Abo.

THE MONKEES

The Monkees, left to right: Davy Jones, Mike Nesmith, Mickey Dolenz and Peter Tork.

Four amenable youths were hired by a Hollywood business conglomerate to play an Anglo-American pop combo in a 1966 television series that was to be networked world-wide. They were also required to mime its musical interludes which would all be taken from discs on which they'd sung to accompaniment by the best session team that money could buy.

Acting, lip-synching and pretending to play instruments, the "group" were instantly successful, even notching up a hit with 'Last Train To Clarksville' prior to the first screening. With the show in full swing, this was followed by an international Number 1 with 'I'm A Believer'. Then came 'Pleasant Valley Sunday', 'Daydream Believer' and enough lesser smashes to outlast the final series in 1968.

The principals were allowed an increasing say in plot development and a movie, *Head*, as well as in the recording studio. This was especially pleasing to Mickey Dolenz, who wrote 'Alternate Title', a UK chart-topper, and the more prolific Mike Nesmith, also a fair country guitarist—who was to forge a second career as a solo artist as the Monkees faded away.

Dolenz and Davy Jones kept the faith during the Seventies with presentations that all but called themselves "the Monkees" until a more legitimate come-back with Peter Tork in the Eighties when reruns of the old programmes struck chords with both pre-teens and their nostalgic parents.

MOODY BLUES

Formed from veterans of several Midlands beat groups, the Moody Blues—Denny Laine (vocals, guitar), Mike Pinder (keyboards), Ray Thomas (woodwinds, percussion), Clint Warwick (bass) and Graeme Edge (drums)—had won an enviable regional popularity when their second 45, 'Go Now', was a world-wide smash in 1965. Later singles were much less successful and the outfit all but broke up with the departures of Warwick and Laine (later in Paul McCartney's Wings) by 1967. However, with the respective recruitments of John Lodge and, more decisively, Justin Haywood, they revived with a vengeance.

Southerner Justin Haywood (far left) composed the Moody Blues' come-back hit, 'Nights In White Satin'.

After 'Nights In White Satin'—the hit 45 from *Days Of Future Passed*, an ambitious concept LP with orchestra—album after platinum album refined a grandiose style so nebulous in scope that such diverse units as Yes, King Crimson and Roxy Music were all cited erroneously as variants of the Moody Blues prototype.

After 1972's *Seventh Sojourn*, the five took a sabbatical for solo albums such as Thomas's *From Mighty Oaks* and other pet projects like Lodge and Haywood's Top 10 single, 'Blue Guitar'. Soon after regrouping for 1978's *Octave*, Pinder was replaced by Patrick Moraz. Since then, gaps between releases have widened—with 3 years between *The Other Side Of Life* and 1989's *Sur La Mer*, albums that sold steadily if in less striking quantities than previous offerings.

VAN MORRISON

George Ivan Morrison was leader of Irish R&B group Them, who twice entered the UK Top 10 in 1965 with 'Baby Please Don't Go' and 'Here Comes The Night'. However, it was a Morrison-penned B-side, 'Gloria', that was to be the outfit's best-remembered number after it became a US "garage band" set work. In 1966, a mismanaged tour of North America was the last straw for Morrison who left Them to fend for themselves. He brooded in his parents' Belfast home before he was invited to New York by producer Bert Berns to record as a solo artist. As well as spawning a million-seller in 'Brown-Eyed Girl', the sessions chronicled a period of transition for Van, best exampled by Them-type arrangements of tracks that were reworked in 1967 when the impressionistic *Astral Weeks* album began his climb to international stardom—despite the sullen figure he cut on stage and in interview, and a rather one-dimensional vocal style.

He thrived as a proficient tunesmith, "poetic" lyricist, clever arranger and in his use of excellent musicians from jazz, folk and classical fields as well as rock. By the Eighties, he was exploring both his Celtic heritage and interest in Scientology with such as *Inarticulate Speech Of The Heart*, 1988's *Irish Heartbeat* (with the Chieftains) and a UK Top 20 hit with 'Whenever God Shines His Light', a duet with Cliff Richard.

The Move 1968. Left to right: Roy Wood, Trevor Burton, Carl Wayne and Bev Bevan.

MOVE/ELO/WIZZARD

Carl Wayne (vocals), Roy Wood (guitar, vocals), Trevor Burton (guitar), Chris Kefford (bass) and Bev Bevan (drums) burst forth from Birmingham in 1967 with an alarming stage act and a run of memorable and imaginative UK hit singles, including a Number 1 with 1968's 'Blackberry Way'. All were composed by Wood who had taken over as lead singer by 1970 when the Move

consisted only of him, Bevan and, from the Idle Race, guitarist Jeff Lynne, who was to rival Wood as chief songwriter when the group evolved into the Electric Light Orchestra by 1972. Augmented with a violinist, two cellists, a keyboard player and a bass guitarist, ELO made its Top 10 début with Lynne's '10538 Overture'. This was followed by the exit of Wood to lead Wizzard, a band of similarly ornate leanings, through many mid-Seventies smashes such as 'See My Baby Jive', 'Angel Fingers' and 'Are You Ready To Rock'.

Meanwhile, ELO had gone from strength to strength—especially in the US where neither the Move nor Wizzard had nurtured more than a cult following. From 1976's *A New World Record* to an apparent finale with *Balance Of Power* a decade later, all ELO releases were special events for the multitudes who flocked to the futuristic stage extravaganzas that tailed off in ratio to Lynne's growing aversion to touring.

NEW YORK DOLLS

David Johansen (vocals), Johnny Thunders (guitar), Rick Rivets (guitar), Arthur Kane (bass) and Billy Murcia (drums) started as Rolling Stones look-alikes in New York's bohemian clubland before Sylvain Sylvain replaced Rivets. With Todd Rundgren at the console, they recorded an eponymous 1972 début album that was a faithful streamlining of an exhilaratingly slipshod stage act built round 'Looking For A Kiss', 'Personality Crisis' and other originals that were reflective of their collective seedy-flash way of life. Indeed, the Dolls were no saints—as exemplified by Kane's alcoholism and the drug-induced death of Murcia during a British tour.

Though an appositely titled second—and last—album, *Too Much Too Soon*, was a step back in guts, and lost them much of their old following, the Dolls' records and nihilistic stance would later be cited as nascent punk, and it is perhaps significant that, on their last legs, they were managed by future Sex Pistols Svengali Malcolm McLaren. His extreme strategies (such as projecting them as communists) could not, however, halt the decline of these titans of trash, unable as they were to relive the homemade passion of earlier days.

NILSSON

There is much division over Harry Edward Nilsson III. Is he an inconsistent genius who defies categorization or a tiresome *bon viveur*, content to have fulfilled only a fraction of his potential?

While holding down a job in a Californian bank, he hawked his songs round Hollywood, and released unsuccessful singles under various aliases. However, a 1967 début album, *Pandemonium Shadow Show*, was praised by the Beatles, and provoked covers of its tracks by such diverse acts as Billy J. Kramer, the Yardbirds and Herb Alpert. A second LP, *Aerial Ballet*, contained 'One', a million-seller when rearranged by Three Dog Night, and

1970 album of Randy Newman numbers. The second half of Nilsson's career was, nevertheless, less impressive than the first. Despite a commercial apogee with 'Without You' (from 1971's *Nilsson Schmilsson*), he became better known for excesses with famous intimates like John Lennon and Keith Moon. Yet he remains one of pop's great enigmas: the much-covered songwriter whose two most enduring recordings were written by others, and the singer who has almost never been before a public audience.

ROY ORBISON

This bespectacled Texan first reached the US Hot 100 in 1956 with 'Ooby Dooby'. Other singles in the same rockabilly style were less successful, unsuited as they were to his powerful quasi-operatic baritone. He had all but retired as a professional musician when, in the same 1958 month, the Everly Brothers and Jerry Lee Lewis had Top 10 entries with Orbison songs as B-sides. He was then engaged as a jobbing composer by Nashville's mighty Acuff-Rose management and publishing firm who also arranged for him to record two flop singles before he re-entered the charts with 'Uptown'. Its follow-up, 'Only The Lonely', was a world-wide smash. Subsequent hits—some with no discernable chorus or hook-line—such as 'Running Scared', 'Cryin'', 'In Dreams' and 1964's almost suicidal 'It's Over' had him typecast as a merchant of melancholy. One of his best remembered songs, however, is the upbeat 'Oh! Pretty Woman'.

Harry Nilsson relaxes during a 1972 recording session.

Nilsson's version of Fred Neil's 'Everybody's Talkin', also used as the theme song for the 1969 film *Midnight Cowboy*. More hits followed, as did movie sound track commissions (and acting roles), and unexpected tangents like a

It has to be said that *part* of Orbison's allure after the mid-Sixties was morbid fascination. Following the death of his first wife and two of his sons in separate calamities, he undertook a strenuous but therapeutic touring schedule as the hits dried up. While his concerts were buoyed by past successes, he continued to release new material, and had made something of a come-back in 1988 when he suffered a fatal heart attack.

PINK FLOYD

See separate entry in the Legends section.

GENE PITNEY

This University of Connecticut graduate was first recognized in the music business as a writer of hits by the likes of Ricky Nelson and Bobby Vee. As a performer, he made a moderate Hot 100 début with 1961's 'Love My Life Away' before climbing higher with two successive film title songs, 'Town Without Pity' and 'The Man Who Shot Liberty Valence'. Further Pitney hits included 'Only Love Can Break A Heart', 'Twenty-Four Hours from Tulsa', 'I'm Gonna Be Strong'—his biggest UK smash apart from a chart-topping duet of 'Something's Gotten Hold Of My Heart' with Marc Almond in 1989— 'Backstage', 'Nobody Needs Your Love' and the 1967 solo blueprint of 'Something's Gotten Hold Of My Heart'.

Without exception, they were all ballads sung in that piercing nasal tenor that you either liked or you didn't.

What couldn't be denied was that short-haired, besuited Pitney was a professional. During, say, an Australian tour, he might be caught off-guard by an abrupt rise of sales in France. He'd then drop everything to fly to Paris for a television spot before dashing back to the interrupted campaign Down Under. By the Seventies, however, such excursions became less frequent as chart entries were coming less easily to him. This did not, however, much bother Pitney who can rely on sell-out concerts until he decides to retire.

POLICE

Though Gordon "Sting" Sumner (vocals, bass), Henri Padovani (guitar) and Stewart Copeland (drums) each adopted a vaguely punk appearance, Copeland and Sumner were steeped in jazz and progressive rock. Preferring musicianship to "attitude", they replaced Padovani in 1977 with Andy Summers who, if nearing middle age, had an impressive pop lineage

The Police, left to right: Stewart Copeland, Andy Summers, Gordon "Sting" Sumner.

that included service with Zoot Money, Soft Machine and the Animals. With a workable line-up waiting for direction, Sumner in particular exploded as a songwriter, providing the outfit with a "sleeper" hit in 'Roxanne' which lit the way for 'Can't Stand Losing You', 'Message In A Bottle' and further smashes—initially in the same reggaefied style—on both sides of the Atlantic.

As well as being the prime source of its teenage appeal, Sumner was also the group's intellectual, as shown by his increasingly more involved lyrics with each successive million-selling album, though he kept a weather eye on the singles market with such as 'Every Little Thing She Does Is Magic' and—also a UK Number 1—1983's 'Every Breath You Take'. His solo projects (which included starring roles in movies) were more successful than those of Copeland and Summers, and to all intents and purposes he had left the Police, who have never officially disbanded, by the mid-Eighties.

ELVIS PRESLEY

See separate entry in the Legends section.

THE PRETENDERS

This post-punk outfit's X-factor was Chrissie Hynde (vocals, guitar, harmonica), a North American who arrived in London in 1976. She was backed by James Honeyman-

Scott (guitar), Pete Farndon (bass) and Martin Chambers (drums). Modest UK chart entries with a revival of the Kinks' 'Stop Your Sobbin', and the self-written 'Kid' were followed by 1979's 'Brass In Pocket' from the same eponymous début album. This went to Number 1, and also slipped into the US Top 20.

If sustained beyond the mid Eighties by further

Chrissie Hynde (left) is a former student of Ohio's Kent State University.

hits like 'I Go To Sleep' and 1986's 'Hymn To Her', the outfit was plagued by grave internal crises, notably the deaths of Honeyman-Scott and Fardon, and Hynde's affair with Ray Davies of the Kinks and consequent pregnancy. Another child would result from a brief marriage to Jim Kerr of Simple Minds. Nevertheless, the group bounced back with replacements similar in style to the departed players, and a less taxing recording schedule, though Hynde found time to team up with UB40 for hit retreads of Sonny And Cher's 'I Got You Babe' and, in 1988, Dusty Springfield's 'Breakfast In Bed'. Her commendable involvement in animal liberation issues led to unlooked-for publicity in 1989 when an off the cuff remark was interpreted by certain press organs as her incitement to firebomb McDonald's burger chain.

PRETTY THINGS

Phil May (vocals) and ex-Rolling Stone Dick Taylor (guitar) formed this London R&B group in 1963. Their abandoned performances and long-haired reprobate image held instant appeal for record company talent scouts looking for an act to combat the Stones. After replacing drummer Viv Andrews with Viv Prince, and testing the chart water with 'Rosalyn', the Pretty Things made the UK Top 20 with the singles 'Don't Bring Me Down' and 'Honey I Need'.

A few minor hits later, they signed off the UK Top 50 forever with 1966's 'House In The Country'. By then, their music had acquired a less derivative sophistication as Taylor and May found their feet as composers, placing a greater emphasis on vocal harmony via the recruitment of new personnel from the ranks of Bern Elliott's Fenmen. However, sales did not match critical acclaim for such as *S.F. Sorrow*, arguably the first "rock opera", and 1969's *Parachute, Rolling Stone* magazine's Album of the Year. The harrowing decade that followed was epitomized by a 3-year lay-off until a solitary Dutch concert sponsored by a fan was stimulating enough for a more permanent reformation that has produced recordings more startling than those of many luckier contemporaries.

QUEEN

Shrugging off indifference towards their early records—one issued under an alias—this London quartet—Freddie Mercury (vocals), Brian May (guitar), John Deacon (bass) and Roger Taylor (drums)—got moving in 1974 when *Queen II* and then its 45, 'Seven Seas Of Rhye' each probed the appropriate UK Top 10s. Progress became even more tangible when the next releases, *Sheer Heart Attack* and 'Killer Queen', took them high up the US chart too. Outliving glam-rock, they reached an artistic apotheosis with 1975's epic 'Bohemian Rhapsody', mostly the work of Mercury, which brought ersatz grand opera to pop (via what was, debatably, the first use of video promotion).

Against this yardstick, later smashes seemed pale, but they were smashes all the same as the outfit explored such diversities as Presley-esque pastiche (with 'Crazy Little Thing Called Love'), film themes (e.g. 1980's *Flash Gordon*) and numerous extramural projects like 'Barcelona', Mercury's hit duet with Monserrat Caballe.

After Mercury's death in 1991, morbid publicity and commercial pragmatism pushed 'Bohemian Rhapsody' back to Number 1. The following April, an all-star London memorial concert to Freddie was satellite-linked to even more millions across the globe than *Live Aid* had been.

THE RAMONES

Soon after a début performance in 1974 by Joey Hyman (vocals, drums), John Cummings (guitar) and Doug Colvin (bass), manager Tommy Erdelyi became drummer so that Hyman could concentrate more on singing. By the time they began recording an eponymous first album in 1976, all members had adopted the "Ramone" stage surname. *The Ramones* and its singles were both praised and denigrated as nascent punk.

By 1979, Erdelyi had retired to the studio. His successor, Marc Bell from the Voidoids, had been heard on lack-lustre *Road To Ruin* and the more vibrant *It's Alive* concert album. He and the others also featured in 1979's *Rock 'N' Roll High School* movie, which preceded a revival of the Ronettes' 'Baby I Love You', their only British Top 10 entry.

With all the qualities of their earlier offerings, 1981's *Pleasant Dreams* and its *Subterranean Jungle* follow-up had few that appealed to the record-buying public. Affairs improved fractionally with further albums, but a world tour with Debbie Harry in 1990 was dismissed by many as akin to a nostalgia revue and did little for their reputation.

The Ramones' 'Sheena Is A Punk Rocker' almost reached the UK Top 20 in 1977.

REM

Michael Stipe (vocals), Peter Buck (guitar), Michael Mills (bass) and Bill Berry (drums) came from the bohemian district of Athens, Georgia, where they played their first concert in 1980. A fondness for Sixties pop was evident from their first releases on small labels and also in the pronounced hand they had in a 1991 Troggs album that was nearly an ersatz REM disc.

Well before they inched into the US album Top 50 with 1983's *Murmur*, they had been critically favoured by all manner of specialist music journals. Their cult standing was consolidated universally with 1984's *Reckoning* hovering in the lower reaches of most world charts. *Fables of The Reconstruction* and *Dead Letter Office* seemed to serve as respective holding operations before and after 1986's *Life's Rich Pageant* edged them nearer the mainstream market with few artistic concessions on their part.

'The One I Love', a 45 from the *Document* follow-up, was the US Top 10 début that finally elevated them from cult luminaries to pop stars. Yet, after an almost cursory world tour in 1989, REM fought shy of the big time, giving 1991's *Out Of Time* little direct promotional aid. However, this did no harm as the album was a US Number 1 for months, creating almost unendurable anticipation among fans for the next one.

REM's *Automatic For The People* (1993) consolidated their standing as reluctant pop stars.

CLIFF RICHARD

With his Nineties concerts mingling strolls down Memory Lane with recent smashes, this vocalist has been a British pop institution since 1959 when, backed by the Shadows and produced by Norrie Paramor, his fifth 45, 'Living Doll', was the first of many UK Number 1s and his only US Top 30 entry until 1976's 'Devil Woman'. Relying more on hired composers than US covers, he was more comfortable as an "English Elvis" than Tommy Steele. Yet he entered the Sixties by following a wholesome "all-round entertainer" path. During the beat boom, he shovelled out a greater proportion of potboiling ballads, and plunged deeper into pantomime, Songs For Europe and evangelical Christianity. Like Presley's, most of his films were quasi-musicals of cheery unreality.

By the Seventies, he could not take hits for granted any more. Therefore, he revamped his musical aspirations with the help of younger minds than the late Paramor's. The three years after 'Devil Woman' were patchy but the tide turned suddenly when, on the heels of two Top 40 flops, 1979's 'We Don't Talk Anymore' put him at the top for the first time since 1968. Chartwise, he endured a couple more "wilderness years" in the mid-Eighties but matters improved again after 1988's 'Mistletoe And Wine' established a tradition of a British Top 10 entry for every Christmas since.

THE ROLLING STONES

See separate entry in the Legends section.

THE SEARCHERS

The Searchers came into being in 1961 as resident trio—Tony Jackson, John McNally, Mike Pender—in a Liverpool tavern. The gifted Chris Curtis was eventually engaged as singing drummer, and Jackson persuaded to switch to electric bass. For a while, they backed C&W vocalist Johnny Sandon until his transference to the better-paid Remo Four obliged the Searchers to share lead vocals and develop the tidy harmonies and restrained fretboard interaction that were to become stylistic trademarks after a 1963 UK Number 1 with 'Sweets For My Sweet' removed them from the Merseyside–Hamburg treadmill. Big hits were forthcoming for another two years, even after the replacement in 1964 of Jackson with Frank Allen from Cliff Bennett's Rebel Rousers

A measure of belated chart success in the States was followed by the exit of Curtis and a turn-around of their commercial fortunes. Years on the cabaret and nostalgia trail were punctuated by two well-received albums of new material in the late Seventies, and an abrupt division in 1986 into two independent factions—"Mike Pender's Searchers" and an "official" Searchers.

THE SEX PISTOLS

See separate entry in the Legends section.

THE SHADOWS

While backing and, later, composing songs for Cliff Richard, Hank B. Marvin (lead guitar), Bruce Welch (rhythm guitar), Jet Harris (bass) and Tony Meehan (drums) recorded independently and became acknowledged generally as Britain's top instrumental act—and Marvin the most omnipotent of British lead guitarists, given those fretboard heroes like Jeff Beck and Ritchie Blackmore who began in Shadows-style units.

The Shadows survived both Merseybeat and the losses of Meehan and the charismatic Harris by producing material at least as good as 'Apache' and anything else prior to 1963, though they recorded a Top 10 vocal concession to the beat boom in 1965's self-penned 'Don't Make My Baby Blue' as disbandment in 1968 loomed.

Marvin, Welch and Bennett had reformed the group with a succession of bass players by 1975 when they returned to the Top 20 with 'Let Me Be The One', a Song For Europe entry. By the Eighties, they had settled down to annual tours and studio albums, with occasional stage reunions with Cliff and even the odd instrumental foray in the singles charts, before once more calling it a day in late 1992.

SHANGRI-LAS

At the zenith of the "British invasion", this New York schoolgirls quartet attempted to cash in as the Bon-Bons with 'What's Wrong With Ringo'. Under their more familiar name, they came under the aegis of producer George "Shadow" Morton who thrust them to the US and UK Top 20s with the brine-washed 'Remember (Walking In The Sand)' before overseeing their *pièce de résistance* 'Leader Of The Pack', a teenage morality play that climaxes with a "fast" boy's fatal motorbike crash amid the extra drama of Morton's collage of snarling engines, squealing rubber *et al*. Less successfully, its mordant theme was investigated from new angles with such as 'I Can Never Go Home Anymore' (their US Top 10 farewell) 'Dressed In Black' and world-weary 'Past Present And Future', though there were fleeting joys like the forces favourite, 'Give Him A Great Big Kiss'. After lead singer Betty Weiss quit in 1967, the other three continued as a trio. Seventies rereleases of 'Leader Of The Pack' climbed the British Top 20. It was revived by the Portsmouth Sinfonia in 1979, by which time Mary Weiss and the Glaser sisters had long been fixtures on US "Sounds of the Sixties"-type presentations.

SLADE

In the late Sixties, Noddy Holder (vocals, guitar), Dave Hill (guitar), Jim Lea (bass, keyboards, violin) and Don Powell (drums) ploughed a "progressive" furrow as Ambrose Slade before pruning both their name and hair when their manager, ex-Animal Chas Chandler, recommended a "skinhead" image. However, when an arrangement of Little Richard's 'Get Down And Get With It' marked their UK Top 20 début, they were glam-rockers whose A-side output was to consist mostly of unremitting ravers (all composed with mostly misspelt titles by Holder and Lea) that would push Slade high up the lists—all the way up on several occasions—until 1974. Indeed, they

racked up more chart entries than the Beatles, even if the number of weeks spent there were less impressive after the golden age of 'Mama Weer All Crazee Now', 'Skweeze Me Pleeze Me' et al. Yet the mid-Eighties were red-letter years with both reissues and latest releases in the UK Top 10 as well as their finally cracking

Slade, left to right: Jim Lea, Dave Hill, Noddy Holder and Don Powell.

the US market after hit revivals of two of their chart-busters by Quiet Riot. Since then, record sales have not followed rhyme or reason, though concerts remained guaranteed sell-outs until Holder's apparent retirement from touring in 1991 hung a question mark over Slade's future.

SMALL FACES

After making the UK Top 20 with 1965's 'Whatcha Gonna Do About It' and suffering a miss with the self-composed 'I Got Mine', this pre-eminent London Mod group—Steve Marriott (vocals, guitar), Ronnie Lane (bass, vocals), Jimmy Winston (keyboards) and Kenny Jones (drums)—replaced Winston with Ian McLagen, and got back on course with 'Sha-La-La-La-Lee', 'Hey Girl' 'All Or Nothing' (their only chart-topper) and lesser hits before touching a post-1967 creative peak with 'Here Come The Nice', 'Itchycoo Park', 'Tin Soldier', and 'Lazy Sunday Afternoon' which summed up the Small Faces' dialectic in its blend of R&B, psychedelia and Cockney chirpiness.

'Itchycoo Park' was the vehicle of a US advance that was thwarted by Marriott's exit for Humble Pie. Jones, Lane and MacLaren carried on as the Faces with Rod Stewart and Ron Wood from the Jeff Beck group, but, though successful, both the Faces and Humble Pie broke up in the mid Seventies, and a Small Faces reunion was a natural regression, particularly as they were one of precious few Sixties acts acceptable to punk. Nevertheless,

as indifference towards two come-back albums against Top 40 placings for repromoted Sixties singles demonstrated, a contemporary rebirth was not feasible, and Marriott's death in 1991 quelled speculation about any more regroupings.

BRUCE SPRINGSTEEN

He made a professional beginning in Steel Mill, a New Jersey bar band, and as a solo singing guitarist before fronting the E Street Band. His first album, 1973's *Greetings From Asbury Park, NJ,* and other early records caused some critics to declare him the new Dylan, though noted pop author Nick Cohn would dismiss him with: "Can't sing. Terrible songs. The world's worst poet." Enough buyers disagreed—"because he passes as a man of the people", snarled Cohn—to put 1975's *Born To Run* LP and single into international charts. With an animated and constantly readjusted stage act, he milked this breakthrough for all it was worth. Later, he'd consolidate his standing by quoting classic rock in his lyrics, lending practical support to has-beens like Gary US Bonds, and proud public familiarity with pop Methuselahs such as Roy Orbison and Ringo Starr. He'd even have the nerve to play up to the notion that he had all it took to usurp Elvis Presley's throne as the King of Rock.

As "the Boss", Bruce did very well out of it. The mid-Eighties were his fattest years with a hat-trick of US album chart-toppers, and publicized altruisms that ranged from his conspicuous hand in *Sun City*—a post-*Live Aid* project that raised over $400,000 for anti-apartheid movements—to a benefit for an old Asbury Park pal down on his luck.

STATUS QUO

After years of struggle under other nomenclatures, London's Status Quo—Mike Rossi (vocals, guitar), Rick Harrison (vocals, guitar), Roy Lynes (keyboards), Alan Lancaster (bass) and John Coghlan (drums)—finally hit pay-dirt with 1968's psychedelic 'Pictures Of Matchstick Men' in both the UK and US Top 20s. Yet apart from another UK smash with 'Ice In The Sun', a series of flops and the correlated exit of Lynes over the next 2 years indicated that the group was on the way out. Abandoning both "progressive" pretensions and attempts to become cabaret entertainers, Quo re-emerged with immense and lasting success as denim-clad blues-boogie merchants—a revision of policy exemplified by Rossi and Harrison's reassumptions of their respective given names of Francis Rossi and Rick Parfitt.

'Break The Rules', 'Down Down', a 1976 revival of Hank Thompson's 'Wild Side Of Life' and other huge sellers made little impression in North America despite the optimistic title bestowed on 1977's single album tour project, *Rockin' All Over The World*, which did just that with a profitable vengeance in other territories. In the Eighties, big hits were less frequent, and personal relationships were often less than harmonious, but Status Quo remain a popular concert attraction, and can still pull unexpected commercial strokes.

STEELEYE SPAN

This folk-rock outfit began in 1970 as a merger of Ashley Hutchings (ex-Fairport Convention bass player) and two folk club duos—Gay and Terry Woods (concertina, vocals, guitar) and Maddy Prior (vocals) and Tim Hart (dulcimer, guitar, vocals)—but the proverbial "musical differences" led to the departure of the more purist Woods couple and the recruitment of Peter Knight (violin, mandolin)

Steeleye Span, a marriage of rustic lyricism and rock-a-boogie.

and well-known ethnic vocalist Martin Carthy before the recording of 1971's *Please To See The King* album.

A more overtly rock determination developed over the next few albums, particularly after the exits of Carthy and Hutchings, and the enrolment of electric guitarist Bob Johnson (who'd once backed Gary Glitter), Rick Kemp on bass and drummer Nigel Pegrum. This bold development culminated in Top 20 hits with 1975's 'Guadette' and 'All Around My Hat' with its marriage of rock-a-boogie and rustic lyricism.

By the time of its unacclaimed disbandment in 1980, the group was starting to drift back to its folk roots to the degree of reinstating Carthy. However, it was the 1975 line-up minus Hart who reunited six years later for *Back In Line* and, bar Kemp, for another album, *Tempted And Tried,* in 1989.

STEPPENWOLF

John Kay (vocals), Michael Monarch (guitar), Goldy McJohn (organ), Rushton Morave (bass) and Jerry Edmonton (drums) worked venues local to Toronto as Sparrow. This nascent hybrid of psychedelia and blues would be heard on *Early Steppenwolf*, an album released after the renamed outfit replaced Morave with John Morgan, and migrated to California. 1968's *Steppenwolf* included million-selling 'Born To Be Wild'. With another track, 'The Pusher', it was also a highlight of 1969's *Easy Rider* film soundtrack.

Like 'Born To Be Wild', the self-penned 'Magic Carpet Ride' (from *The Second*) stopped one place short of topping the US Hot 100, and 1969's 'Rock Me' (from the movie *Candy*) also reached the Top 10. Nevertheless, squabbles during the recording of *At Your Birthday Party* ended with the recruitment of new personnel in guitarist Larry Byron and bass player Nick St Nicholas to contribute to 1970's *Monster* before they were supplanted themselves by George Biondi and Kent Henry. After the *Live* album fell from international charts, the group remained a huge concert draw but ebbing record sales led to disbandment in 1974. Though the 1972 edition reformed briefly two years later, Kay was the only original member present when Steppenwolf reared up again in 1990.

ROD STEWART

On leaving the Raiders in 1961, an initially desultory professional career was marked by flop singles and periods with various British R&B/soul acts including Jimmy Powell And The Five Dimensions and Steampacket. In 1968, Rod Stewart landed a prestigious job as lead vocalist with the Jeff Beck Group. Malcontented under Beck's leadership, he and guitarist Ron Wood joined the Small Faces who had been at a loss following the resignation of singing guitarist Steve Marriott. As just plain Faces, their Top 20 strikes on both sides of the Atlantic were enhanced by knockabout stage routines and the greater success of Stewart's solo records such as 1971's international chart-topper, the self-written 'Maggie May' from the million-selling *Every Picture Tells A Story*.

A mixture of economics and artistic frustration led Stewart to strike out entirely on his own in 1975. This decision was to prove correct through continued chart triumphs with a wide range of material—revivals of Tamla-Motown hits, a soccer anthem, folk-rock, movie themes, you name it—all filtered through an unmistakable husk of a voice that can still conjure up a mental picture of shock-headed Rod as a womanizing jack-the-lad, an image that survives despite a middle-aged joviality and a happy second marriage.

STONE ROSES

Like the Rolling Stones, whose name seemed to have inspired their own, and the Sex Pistols (a main influence on singer Ian Brown and guitarist John Squire's previous group, the Patrol) this Manchester combo put themselves forward as rock's bad boys, from graffiti publicity campaigns when they formed in 1985 to wantonly damaging record company offices to sniping at the monarchy in disc grooves. Their musical meat was a hybrid of psychedelia and the quasi mechanical dance rhythms popular in local discos. After the replacement of Andrew Cousins (bass), *The Stone Roses* crept into the UK album Top 40, as did their sixth single, 1989's self-composed 'She Bangs The Drums', in its chart. The next 45, 'Fool's Gold', peaked at Number 8. An earlier single, 'Sally

The Stone Roses: brand leaders of Manchester pop in the Eighties.

Cinnamon', was then reissued to bridge the gap before 1990's 'One Love' reached the Top 5.

These entries were a surface manifestation of the outfit's power as a concert attraction. This pervaded North America where, after an impolite refusal of a support spot on a Rolling Stones tour, they made a promising start by nurturing a following big enough to put their album in the lower half of the US list for 4 months. However, the demise of Manchester as a pop centre has not helped further progress.

THE STRANGLERS

This group from Surrey, UK—Hugh Cornwell (guitar, vocals), Jean-Jacques Burnel (bass, vocals), Dave Greenfield (keyboards) and Jet Black (drums)—had endured some years of hard graft on the road before finding favour with punk with their saturnine image, quarrelsome attitude towards the media, hard-man lyrics and update of the Doors' musical style. After 1977's 'Peaches' made the UK Top 10, they saw punk out with further smashes promoted during engagements marked by provocative (and sometimes self-destructive) on-stage dialogue and antics that stirred up a frequent violent reaction from their audiences.

When the punk storm passed, they toured less often, and toned down the aggression in disc output after testing the Top 40 water with a 1978 version of Dionne Warwick's limp 'Walk On By'. Almost topping the British charts in 1982, the self-composed 'Golden Brown' was in the same gentle vein, though it was castigated as being a paean to heroin in the light of Cornwell's jailing two years earlier for possession of same. By the later Eighties, the quartet were falling back more than ever before on revivals of old songs. Cornwell's resignation in 1990 might have been a suitable point to disband but, replacing him with look-alike Pat Roberts, his colleagues carried on regardless.

STRAY CATS

Though it was in Britain that they found most chart success, these New Yorkers—Brian Setzer (vocals, guitar), Lee Rocker (double bass) and Slim Jim Phantom (drums)—surfaced as North America's chief contribution to the brief but intense rockabilly renaissance in the early Eighties. As well as self-composed material and the expected Fifties items, the trio's repertoire also embraced Creedence Clearwater Revival and the wilder modern C&W stars.

The most unprecedented tangent, however, was an adaptation of the Supremes' 'You Can't Hurry Love' as the flip-side of 1981's 'Rock This Town'. Two years after it reached the UK Top 10, it did likewise in the States where an LP hastily compiled from their first two UK albums sold over 2 million units. However, after 'Rock This Town', only 'Runaway Boys', 'Stray Cat Strut', 'The Race Is On' (a collaboration with Dave Edmunds, their producer) and 'Sexy And 17' were to make anything approaching major impact before the group disbanded in 1983. Phantom and Rocker then teamed up with US guitarist Earl Slick before reuniting with Setzer to record 1989's *Blast Off* and its spin-off single, 'Bring It Back Again'. Both made fleeting appearances in their respective lists in Britain.

THIN LIZZY

The "progressive" substance of their first two albums—1970's *Thin Lizzy* and *Shades Of A Blue Orphanage*—was at odds with the hard rock content of the stage act that made Phil Lynott (vocals, bass), Eric Bell (guitar) and Brian Downey (drums) a reliable draw beyond the pale of their native Dublin, before a migration to London in 1972 and the replacement of Bell with Gary Moore, who was soon superseded himself by two guitarists in Brian Robertson (ex-Average White Band) and Scott Gorman. In 1973, the quartet's rocked-up version of the traditional 'Whiskey In The Jar' eased into the UK Top 10, thereby generating interest in *Vagabonds Of The Western World*, which, like the succeeding *Nightlife* and *Fighting*, shifted many copies over a long period without actually figuring in the album Top 40. Another hit single, 'The Boys Are Back In Town', however, pushed its album, 1976's *Jailbreak*, high up the list. It also took off in North America. Despite Robertson's exit necessitating the hiring of a succession of temporary guitarists, the band's 1976 advance swelled to a commercial peak in the later Seventies. Their records continued to sell well until the late Lynott—the main creative force—elected to devote more energy to a parallel solo career that had begun with 1980's appositely titled *Solo In Soho* album.

The Tornados, 1964: drummer Clem Cattini (far right) now leads a 1993 edition of the group.

THE TORNADOS

George Bellamy (guitar), Alan Caddy (guitar), Roger Lavern (keyboards), Heinz Burt (bass) and Clem Cattini (drums) were Billy Fury's backing combo before independent producer Joe Meek employed them in 1961 as an all-purpose ensemble to accompany discs by artists such as John Leyton, notably on that year's 'Johnny Remember Me' chart-topper. Writing much of their material, Meek also recorded them as a self-contained entity. After a flop with 'Love And Fury', the Tornados raced to Number 1 with 1962's 'Telstar', which did likewise in the US Hot 100 where an attendant LP sold well too. Further US progress was checked when executive politics caused the cancellation of a tour.

Three more 45s made 1963's UK Top 20 before the Tornados became *passé* with the coming of Merseybeat. Sales dwindled too through the exit of Viking-featured Burt for a career as a solo singer, and releases that either repeated old ideas or made token concessions to current trends.

They disbanded soon after the 1967 suicide of their console Svengali—though the 'Telstar' line-up were to play a few nostalgia bookings in the mid Seventies. A more permanent reformation occurred in 1989 with a Tornados led by drummer Clem Cattini as the only original member of one of the great British instrumental groups of the Sixties.

TRAFFIC

From various unsuccessful Midlands outfits, Jim Capaldi (drums, vocals), Dave Mason (vocals, guitar, bass) and Chris Wood (woodwinds) gladly teamed up with the gifted Steve Winwood (vocals, keyboards, guitar),

former linchpin of the Spencer Davis Group, who was to have the full entrepreneurial support of Island Records. His new group, said the press office, would "get it together" in a remote rural cottage. That two singles—'Paper Sun' and 'Hole In My Shoe'—and the *Dear Mr Fantasy* album all made their respective UK Top 10s demonstrated the benefit of this alleged collaboration. However, tensions between Mason and Winwood led the former to quit Traffic in 1968, an exit that was

among causes of the band's split in the New Year. Yet, following Wood and Capaldi's ample assistance during its sessions, an intended solo offering by Winwood came to be issued in 1970 as a Traffic album, *John Barleycorn Must Die!*

Augmented by other musicians, the group reached a commercial summit with 1971's million-selling *Low Spark Of High-Heeled Boys* before an over-reliance on long-winded improvisations failed to mask creative bankruptcy on the *Shoot Out At The Fantasy Factory* follow-up and the in-concert *On The Road*, though a return to form with 1974's *When The Eagle Flies* finale intimated that, had Traffic continued, it may well have "got it together" again.

THE TROGGS

Before this Hampshire outfit's first single, 1965's 'Lost Girl', guitarists Dave Wright and Howard Mansfield were replaced by Chris Britton and Pete Staples (bass) to enable the previous bass player, Reg Ball, to front the Troggs as lead vocalist. Finer tuning was the work of manager Larry Page, as shown by his giving Ball and drummer Ronnie Bullins the more impressive-sounding surnames of Presley and Bond when a second single, 'Wild Thing', charged towards the top of the UK chart in 1966; its follow-up, 'With A Girl Like You', actually seizing the

Traffic in 1967. Clockwise from top left: Jim Capaldi, Steve Winwood, Dave Mason and (seated) Chris Wood.

The Troggs. Left to right: Pete Staples, Reg Presley, Ronnie Bond and Chris Britton.

Number 1 spot, and 'I Can't Control Myself' (another Presley composition) almost doing the same in autumn. These early discs sold millions in North America too, but momentum was lost through administrative wrangles. However, the recurrence of Troggs numbers in the repertoires of countless US "garage bands", and their own success in other regions—with the subdued 'Any Way That You Want Me' in late 1966 to a South African Number 1 with 1972's 'Feels Like A Woman'—were a solid foundation for a lucrative post-Top 40 career that has embraced many intriguing releases such as a small UK solo hit by the late Bond in 1980, and a link-up with REM for 1991's *Athens To Andover* album.

U2

As Feedback, a Dublin school band, Paul "Bono" Hewson (vocals), David "the Edge" Evans (guitar), Adam Clayton (bass) and Larry Mullen (drums) were nothing special until they "went punk" in 1976. They'd become U2 when a run of national hits began in 1979, but it was to be another 2 years before they made the slightest headway in the UK. However, after 'New Year's Day' swept into its Top 10 in January 1983, there followed a bigger triumph when *War* topped the album charts, as did 1984's *The Unforgettable Fire*, produced by Brian Eno. This was the vehicle of greater success in North America, consolidated when a spot on *Live Aid* affirmed U2's might as a live act on the boards.

Though the punk passion was still discernible on such as 1987's *The Joshua Tree* and 'The Fly'—a UK Number 1 in 1992—the group had cultivated an increasingly more complex style that the vital US market accepted, even welcomed, more immediately than other territories. Moreover, U2 got more highbrow on discovering and absorbing the works of older pop icons like John Lennon, Bob Dylan, Roy Orbison, B. B. King and even Cole Porter—an admiration reciprocated by those among them still alive as the lads who were Feedback entered their thirties ensconced in the rock establishment that they may have once despised.

VELVET UNDERGROUND

Lou Reed (vocals, guitar), Sterling Morrison (guitar), John Cale (keyboards, viola, bass) and Maureen Tucker (drums) had a repertoire that hinged on composer Reed's perspectives on his native New York's *demi-monde*. Some would be sung by Nico, a German actress who joined at the insistence of pop-art pioneer Andy Warhol, who let the combo rehearse in his Factory studio and incorporated them into his Exploding Plastic Inevitable troupe. In 1966 came the sensational *Velvet Underground And Nico* with its unprecedented coverage of drug addiction, sexual taboos and mental instability. While Reed's emotional vocabulary on this album was to ripple across decades of pop, the Nico-less follow-up, *White Light White Heat,* was more Cale's baby, being less reliant on individual items than sound at any given moment.

Rows with Reed led to Cale's replacement by Doug Yule for 1969's subdued *The Velvet Underground*. Yule was allowed a few lead vocals on 1970's *Loaded*, and his drumming brother, Billy, was brought in to cover Tucker's maternity leave. Before *Loaded* reached the shops, Reed left for a solo career. His subsequent work, however successful, was always measured against his music with the Velvet Underground who, without him, folded after one album, 1972's *Squeeze*.

In 1993 the original members (minus the late Nico) regrouped for a European tour.

SCOTT WALKER/WALKER BROTHERS

After several flop records and a spell as bass player with the Routers, an instrumental combo, Ohio-born singer Scott Engel teamed up with John Maus (vocals, guitar) and Gary Leeds (drums). As the Walker Brothers, they sought their fortunes in Britain where their second single, 'Love Her', made the Top 20 in 1965. Then came bigger smashes with 'Make It Easy On Yourself', 'My Ship Is Coming In', 'The Sun Ain't Gonna Shine Any More' and like orchestral ballads with Engel on lead vocals as the trio emerged as the darlings of young ladies in the UK and, to a smaller degree, in the States. However, provoked by both bickering between Engel and Maus and falling sales, the Brothers went separate ways in 1967.

Engel's *Scott* and 1968's chart-topping *Scott 2* albums established him as both the Belgian songwriter Jacques Brel's principal interpreter and as an intriguing composer in his own right, but neither these nor *Scott 3* and *Scott 4* were the stuff of mainstream pop, and a cynical Engel was churning out easy-listening potboilers before a reformed Walker Brothers scored a UK hit in 1976 with *No Regrets*. There followed three contrasting albums before Engel resumed a snail-paced solo career with 1984's challenging *Climate Of Hunter*.

Scott Walker waits in the wings.

93

CLIFFORD WHITE

Purists regard him as Britain's foremost exponent of New Age rock. Certainly, this self-taught musician's albums are the ones most often heard hovering in the background in hip painting studios, dental surgeries, health food stores, massage parlours, meditation and improvised dance classes, and in what used to be known as "head shops". Adjectives like "restful", "caressing" and "atmospheric" crop up in critiques of White's unhurried keyboard-dominated instrumentals which, not designed to "go anywhere", were inspired by a combination of his captivation with the Seventies works of Vangelis and Mike Oldfield, and attendance at a Mind, Body and Spirit festival.

With pianist Jon Land, he opened an eight-track studio where *Ascension*—the first of an album trilogy—was recorded in 1984. Through outlets that were not chart-return shops, it sold in vast quantities throughout Europe and North America, principally by word of mouth. Though functioning in a sphere supposed to preclude stardom, Top 20 entries of mystical bent by the Clannad-Enya family and, later, Enigma caused White to mull over contracts offered by major record companies, and venture closer to mainstream pop via 1992's *The Lifespring*.

THE WHO

'I'm The Face', the first single by suburban Londoners Roger Daltrey (vocals), Pete Townshend (guitar), John Entwistle (bass) and Keith Moon (drums), was attributed to the High Numbers before they reverted to their original name for 1965's 'I Can't Explain', 'Anyway Anyhow Anywhere', 'My Generation' and other UK hits that made them the toast of would-be Mods when aligned to a stage act fraught with smoke bombs, flashing lights, splintered instruments and feedback lament. Though Entwistle's macabre, cynical songs were a most agreeable aspect of the Who, Townshend's compositions were what kept the group in the Top 10, on and off, from the post-Mod era until the Eighties. His *Tommy* remains the best-known "rock opera" (actually, a song-cycle) with 1973's *Quadrophenia* a close second.

Moon's principal assets were his publicity-grabbing tomfoolery and the fact that he drummed like a rhythmically integrated octopus. Yet his death in 1978 did not spell the end of the band who continued with ex-Small Face Kenny Jones through a "Mod revival" and then the period of long lay-offs and collective creative decline that culminated in a 1989 world tour when, with no new record in the shops, they milked nostalgia by fixing solely and unashamedly on their back catalogue.

The Who. Clockwise from top left: John Entwistle, Roger Daltrey, Pete Townshend and the late Keith Moon.

JOHNNY AND EDGAR WINTER

These albino brothers played together in Texan R&B outfit Black Plague until Edgar quit to pursue a jazzier path. When singing guitarist Johnny amassed a huge regional following, a 1969 eulogy in the influential *Rolling Stone* journal made him nationally famous. With a début album in the Top 30, he plunged into an exhausting schedule as a headlining act with a backing band that included, on saxophone and keyboards, Edgar who was to quit in 1971 to lead his own Edgar Winter Group to international chart success, notably with a 1972 instrumental, 'Frankenstein'.

Meanwhile, territories beyond North America had also latched on to 1971's *Johnny Winter* and an in-concert collection on which the most thrilling moments were the fretboard duels between Winter and second guitarist Rick Derringer (ex-McCoys). However, irked by declining musical standards and Johnny's interrelated drug dependency, Rick and the other players switched their allegiance to the steadier Edgar for three mid-Seventies albums before the brothers joined forces on 1976's one-off *Together*. Edgar then retreated to studio work, and Johnny became a prominent accompanist to black blues legends while continuing to release workmanlike solo albums, of which 1987's *Third Degree* received most critical acclaim.

STEVE WINWOOD

From his earliest teens, this singing British guitarist and keyboard player was appearing regularly with his father's Midlands dance band and his elder brother's jazz outfit. His distinctive blues-tinged vocal style came to be the main selling-point of the Spencer Davis Group's many UK smashes—'Keep On Running', 'Somebody Help Me' *et al*—and it was this outfit's ill-fortune that he quit just as 1966's 'Gimme Some Lovin' entered the US Top 10. The boy wonder was to dominate Traffic and the short-lived Blind Faith "supergroup" before commencing a solo recording career with an eponymous 1977 album that was something of a false dawn. Matters improved both commercially and artistically with 1981's *Arc Of A Diver* which, instrumentally, was all Winwood's own superimposed work, bequeathing it a lean attack that was also notable on its successor, *Talking Back To The Night*. The one-man-band production criteria were not applied, however, to 1986's Grammy-winning *Back In The High Life* or its chart-topping US single, 'Higher Love'. Both the *Roll With It* follow-up and 1990's *Refugees Of The Heart* were less immediately impressive but, true to precedent, each sped to Number 1 in the States, with sales elsewhere assisted by Winwood covering as many prestigious venues as possible during the necessary world tours.

THE YARDBIRDS

See separate entry in the Legends section.

FRANK ZAPPA

See separate entry in the Legends section.

ZOMBIES

After replacing Paul Arnold (bass) with Chris White, Colin Blunstone (vocals), Paul Atkinson (guitar), Rod Argent (keyboards) and Hugh Grundy (drums) from Hertfordshire, UK, won a local talent contest which led to a recording contract. From this came a début single, 1964's 'She's Not There', which nestled uneasily among more extrovert offerings of the day in the UK Top 20. This triumph was, however, dampened by two successive flops in 'Leave Me Be' and 'Tell Her No'. Yet as booking fees at home dwindled, 'She's Not There' topped the US Hot 100 and smaller hits like 'She's Coming Home' and 'I Want You Back' followed at the height of the "British invasion".

This winning streak was staggered to varying degrees in other territories but, by 1966, the group were driven to block off a rich seam of internal songwriting resources for cynical covers of US smashes.

The Zombies had actually broken up when 1969's 'Time Of The Season' put them at a US Number 3, with commensurate sales for its *Odessey And Oracle* album. Nothing, however, could cajole them to reform, though Argent's eponymous new combo was regarded at first as an ersatz Zombies, and Blunstone (under a pseudonym) returned to the UK Top 40 in 1969 with a remake of the much-covered 'She's Not There'. Indeed, he and Argent each clocked up more chart entries in the Seventies but neither left as insidious a legacy to pop as he had when one of the Zombies.

The Zombies sharing a joke.

97

BEACH BOYS

WEAVERS OF THE CALIFORNIA DREAM

★ ★ ★

Mike Love *(vocals)*, Al Jardine *(vocals, guitar)*,
Carl Wilson *(vocals, guitar)*, Brian Wilson *(vocals, bass)*,
Dennis Wilson *(vocals, drums)*
Formed: Los Angeles, California, USA, 1961

WHO WILL EVER UNRAVEL THE EMOTIONAL COMPLEXITIES OF THE RELATIONSHIP BETWEEN THE BLOOD COUSIN AND THE THREE BROTHERS WHO, WITH JARDINE, FORMED THE GROUP IN LOS ANGELES IN 1961?

Into the bargain, they were managed initially by the Wilsons' father, an amateur songwriter, who pulled strings to secure a contract with Capitol after the outfit had scored a regional hit with 'Surfin'', a ditty that gave only the merest clue of the soaring, interweaving vocal harmonies, topped with Brian Wilson's falsetto, that were to be both much-copied and incomparable.

They climbed the US Top 40 with the likes of 'Surfin' Safari', 'Surfin' USA' and spin-off albums—composed mainly by Brian with Love and other lyricists like Roger Christian who assisted with '409', 'Little Deuce Coupe' *et al* when the Boys rode the crest of the hot-rod craze too. The Boys moved on to less specific areas with such as 1964's 'Fun Fun Fun' and 'I Get Around'— their international Top 10 breakthrough—before Brian chose to concentrate on writing and production back in California while the others continued a hectic touring schedule with a permanent replacement in Bruce Johnston.

While the eldest Wilson still came up with smashes like 1965's 'Help Me Rhonda'—the second US Number 1—and 'California Girls', neither record company moguls nor his collegues minded. If ever the clever stuff with its tempo changes and counterpoint proved weak commercially, the balance could be redressed with a revival of, say, the Regents' 'Barbara Ann', or old folk songs like fast-selling 'Sloop John B', the only non-original on *Pet Sounds*, the most critically acclaimed if least joyous album thus far.

Creating a recurring mood—a "concept", if you like—*Pet Sounds* was inspirational to the Beatles as they prepared *Sgt. Pepper's Lonely Hearts Club Band*. This, in turn, jarred Brian's fragile confidence, even if his Beach Boys had beaten their English rivals in the *New Musical Express*'s 1966 popularity poll, largely through the million-selling 'Good Vibrations', Brian's "pocket symphony". This and its 'Heroes And Villains' follow-up were part of *Smile*, a masterwork that would be abandoned by Brian who had developed severe psychological problems.

Excerpts from *Smile* would serve as selling points on later albums on which other personnel came to the

The Beach Boys less Brian. Clockwise from left: Mike Love, Bruce Johnstone, Carl Wilson, Al Jardine, Dennis Wilson.

fore as songwriters. Nevertheless, by the Seventies, the only merchandise the group could bank on were the greatest hits compilations, even if 1971's *Surf's Up* (with a *Smile* item as its title track) addressed itself to pressing issues such as pollution and left-wing unrest, ensuring that the Beach Boys was a name to drop in hip circles for a while.

There followed an expensive relocation to Amsterdam where 1972's *Holland* was recorded. Though this reinforced their standing as contemporary contenders, Capitol's repackaging strategy adversely affected its sales—as it would all its successors.

The group fought back with a premature reinstatement of Brian in the producer's chair for two patchy mid-Seventies albums before he went into another decline and eventual estrangement from the group.

Receiving more favourable reviews was 1977's *Pacific Ocean Blue*, a solo LP by Dennis Wilson who was to be suspended from the group for general unreliability just before his drowning in 1983. Ringo Starr was among a pool of guest drummers that got the group through an eponymous 1984 album and existing stage dates, thus affirming the respect felt within the music industry for the Beach Boys. Yet if still capable of a surprise US chart-topper with 1988's 'Kokomo', it is these ancient mariners' more enduring past achievements with Brian Wilson that guarantees them seats above the salt in rock's Valhalla.

THE BEATLES

THE MOPTOP MERSEY MARVELS

★ ★ ★

George Harrison *(vocals, guitar)*,
John Lennon *(vocals, guitar)*, Paul McCartney *(vocals, guitar)*,
Ringo Starr *(drums)*
Formed: Liverpool, UK, 1960
Disbanded: London, UK, 1971

THE SHOWBUSINESS SENSATION OF THE CENTURY BEGAN AS JUST ONE OF MANY LIVERPOOL BEAT GROUPS THAT WORKED PUNISHING SCHEDULES IN SEEDY LOCAL DANCE HALLS AND PROVIDED BACKING FOR SOLO PERFORMERS. MANY REMARKABLE COINCIDENCES HELPED THE WHEELS OF THE UNIVERSE TO COME TOGETHER AT THE RIGHT TIME, BUT THEIR SUCCESS WAS NO HAPPY ACCIDENT.

Harrison once suggested that they were an English grammar school interpretation of rock 'n' roll, and the line-up that got through a Hamburg season in 1960 was certainly all from this type of institution. Partly because of their "intellectual" affectations, they were derided as unprofessional poseurs in some quarters. Top-heavy with guitarists, they endured a baptism of much heckling and even beatings-up but they learnt how to tune hostile audiences in to their awry absurdity, eliciting a wildly infectious atmosphere.

In 1961 they acquired a painfully committed manager in Brian Epstein who smartened them up, clarified their image and arranged record company auditions. George Martin, head of an EMI subsidiary, took them on in 1962, just before the replacement of original drummer Pete Best with Ringo Starr (alias Richard Starkey) from Rory Storm And The Hurricanes.

A début single, 'Love Me Do', was the tip of John and Paul's highly commercial songwriting iceberg. Over the next 8 years, the two were to cover all stylistic waterfronts from schmaltz to avant-garde after a prosy *Sunday Times* article lauded them as "the outstanding composers of 1963". That year had also ended with seven Beatles discs in the singles chart and the top two positions on the LP list.

"Beatlemania" was seen by the media as an antidote to months of the Profumo scandal, the Great Train Robbery and similar "heavy" news. "Our appeal", pontificated Starr, "is that we're ordinary lads"—which, as it had in Britain, did the corrective trick in a USA depressed by its own traumas—notably the Kennedy assassination. Launched with a huge publicity blitz, the group were received in North America with an enthusiasm that left British Beatlemaniacs swallowing dust. So insatiable—and uncritical—was demand for anything on which the "Fab Four" had ever breathed that they would account for

The Beatles in 1965. Left to right: George, Paul, John and, seated at the drums, Ringo.

60 per cent of record sales in the States over a 12-month period.

With the surrender of America, everywhere else succumbed too but, for its conquistadores, the world was an intrusive and frequently danger-ous place. A particularly nerve-racking trek round the States in 1966 was followed by a much-mooted decision to cease touring.

Emotional and artistic bonds between personnel loosened. This inevitability was exacerbated the following year by Epstein's sudden death, and vehement critical reaction to the self-produced *Magical Mystery Tour*, an interesting-but-boring tele-vision spectacular, influenced by psychedelia and flirtations with mat-ters mystical, spiritual and fashion

ably precious that altered previous-ly-held public notions of the Beatles as innocent mop-topped scamps.

While still shifting parameters of rock's artistic consciousness, less attractive now was the Beatles' inclination to enact what their minds hadn't formulated in simple terms. Hence the "controlled weirdness" of the multi-faceted Apple Corps, jet-tisoned after their carelessness over expenditure led to a welter of wastefulness, stayed only by the ruthlessness of US accountant Allen Klein who all Beatles but McCartney accepted as Epstein's successor.

Long before Messrs Harrison, Lennon, McCartney and Starr were disassociated formally as a business enterprise in 1971, Japanese per-formance artist Yoko Ono had super-seded McCartney as Lennon's artis-tic collaborator. Meanwhile the Beatles vacillated between the colour supplement art of the *Sgt. Pepper's Lonely Hearts Club Band* album and vain endeavours to get back to their Merseybeat womb.

DAVID BOWIE

IDOL ON PARADE

★ ★ ★

Singer/Songwriter/Actor
Born: January 8, 1947, London, UK

AFTER DAVID ROBERT JONES FINALLY MADE IT IN THE EARLY SEVENTIES, HE KEPT HIS PUBLIC GUESSING BY STAYING SO FAR AHEAD OF THE PACK IN ANTICIPATING TRENDS THAT HE BEGAN INSTIGATING THEM HIMSELF. HOVERING FOR SO LONG ON STRONG CURRENTS, HE BECAME A PAST MASTER AT PULLING UNEXPECTED STROKES WHENEVER CRITICS WERE JUST ABOUT TO WRITE HIM OFF.

Raised in the UK where London bleeds into Kent, he didn't have much going for him in the early Sixties. He honked saxophone well enough to get by in his first group, the Kon-Rads, but wasn't up to making a transition from their chart pop copies to modern jazz. He could find his way round guitar and keyboards, and possessed a tuneful if wobbly voice. His first attempts at songwriting aroused little enthusiasm. Truly, he wasn't a genius musician, or a genius anything in those days, but that didn't matter because he had an indefinable something else.

When the beat boom came by, he made various flop singles as front man of the King Bees, the Manish Boys and then the Lower Third. He reached much the same impasse after he adopted both his familiar stage alias and much of the persona of singing actor Anthony Newley. He also scratched a living as a mime artist, a film extra and by running an arts lab. Perseverance was rewarded in 1969 with a "sleeper" Top 10 entry for 'Space Oddity', a "mini solo opera"—as one reviewer put it—and a pertinent artefact of the year when Neil Armstrong took his small step.

If regarded generally as a one-hit-wonder, regular record releases kept him in the public eye if not the Top 50, especially when he dressed up as a lady for the sleeve of 1971's *The Man Who Sold The World*.

The follow-up, *Hunky Dory*, brought a hit by proxy when Peter "Herman" Noone covered 'Oh! You Pretty Things' (with Bowie on piano) but it was a *Melody Maker* interview in which he made out he was bisexual that prodded the right nerve to get him back into the charts in his own right—with 'Starman' and its album, *The Rise And Fall Of Ziggy Stardust And The Spiders From Mars* which was preoccupied with connections between stardom, madness and—perhaps metaphorical—death. Bowie sustained the breakthrough by assuming the outrageous

Ziggy character on stage before killing it off in time for 1973's *Aladdin Sane.*

Next up was *Pin-Ups,* an affectionate trawl through Sixties beat group preferences, which he plugged on a US television special in 1974. He hammered the States harder with an elaborate stage presentation to accompany the marketing of *Diamond Dogs,* an album that intimated a deep absorption of Orwell's *1984.* However, before this trek wound down, it had metamorphosed into an ersatz soul revue— a fair indication of the direction Bowie was to pursue on *Young Americans* and, to a lesser degree, *Station To Station,* with a front cover taken from Bowie's starring role in *The Man Who Fell To Earth,* a film that was among many ventures into drama by Bowie who, though more than competent, was not the Sir Henry Irving he may have supposed himself to be.

1978's *Just A Gigolo* was shot in Berlin where Bowie dwelt during the recording—with assistance from Brian Eno—of an album trilogy, *Low,*

'Heroes' and *The Lodger,* in which kraut-rock was a pervading influence, though *The Lodger* was the commencement of a gradual return to the rock mainstream, climaxing with 1983's 'Let's Dance', an international chart-topper and, that same year, a US concert for which he was paid a million dollars, cash in hand.

His albums in the later Eighties have been mostly pot-pourris of styles previously tried—a *Young Americans* riff here, an Anthony Newley mannerism there—and the most commercially successful singles were those associated with specific projects as shown by his *Live Aid* 'Dancing In The Street' duet with Mick Jagger and title theme to 1986's *Absolute Beginners* movie.

In 1989, he went off on his most astonishing tangent yet as lead singer and rhythm guitarist of Tin Machine. His name was given no special prominence on billings for engagements to promote the combo's two albums,

which combined hard rock and experiments with tonality. He ratified this new beginning with the extreme gesture of a world tour as a solo attraction performing nothing but old favourites on the understanding that he'd never play them live again.

David displays quiet good taste.

BOB DYLAN

A MAN CALLED "ALIAS"

★ ★ ★

Singer/Songwriter/Guitarist/Harmonica Player
Born: May 24, 1941, Duluth, Minnesota, USA

THE SINGLE MOST ENIGMATIC AND MESSIANIC SYMBOL OF HIPNESS USED TO BE ROBERT ALLEN ZIMMERMAN FROM MINNESOTA BEFORE HE TOOK HIS CHANCES IN NEW YORK'S GREENWICH VILLAGE AS A FOLK PERFORMER.

He was a fair guitarist and harnessed mouth-organist but it was the hideous charm of a humble vocal endowment that got him a CBS recording contract in 1962. His first four albums mingled mostly semi-traditional material and self-written "protest" items, though 1964's *Another Side Of Bob Dylan* seemed to shrug off previous earnestness in tracks like 'My Back Pages'.

There was a howl of derision from folk purists but things got worse for them with 1965's transitional *Bringing It All Back Home* on which Dylan was accompanied for most of it by a beat group as he betrayed unacceptable rock 'n' roll influences. The album also contained 'Mr Tambourine Man', a useful demo for the Byrds who pruned it down to one verse and two choruses for their first Number 1, while Them tackled 'It's All Over Now Baby Blue' and the Walker Brothers covered 'Love Minus Zero'.

On stage, Dylan would revert to his acoustic beginnings for part of the set but the rest would be filled with an amplified recital with the Hawks (later,

the Band) who'd been equally at ease backing Arkansas rock 'n' roller Ronnie Hawkins. Various Hawks joined organist Al Kooper and Nashville session musicians on *Highway 61 Revisited* and 1966's *Blonde On Blonde*, both pivotal to any serious study of both Dylan's music and modern lyric poetry. As it was with *Bringing It All Back Home,* they also provided hits for Dylan himself (including 'Like A Rolling Stone', 'Positively Fourth Street' and 'I Want You') and others, notably Manfred Mann with 'Just Like A Woman'. By then, no one was booing Dylan for "going electric"— very much the opposite.

Off stage, he grew as heartily sick of explaining his surreal songs as the Rolling Stones were of questions about haircuts. Existing merely to vend entertainment with a side-serving of cheap insight became a bore, the adulation intolerable, and some cynics wondered whether his near-fatal motorbike crash in 1966 had actually taken place.

During the shadowy refuge from fame that the accident provided,

Dylan's influence was acknowledged by every rock act that mattered, and his lyrics quoted like proverbs. He became as unreachable an object of myth as Elvis. Hidden away in upstate New York, he and the Band concocted the celebrated *Basement Tapes*, relaxed recordings that were covered extensively long before their official release in 1975.

A water-testing re-emergence on stage at a Woody Guthrie Memorial

Bob Dylan blows up a storm on the Rolling Thunder tour.

Concert in 1968 was followed by *John Wesley Harding* and countrified *Nashville Skyline*, albums more understated and lyrically direct than Dylan's mid Sixties offerings— though the former's 'All Along The Watchtower' lent itself to adventurous interpretations by others.

Excerpts from a merely competent 60-minute show at 1969's Isle of Wight Pop Festival—Dylan's first major appearance since his motorcycle calamity—were included on 1970's iconoclastic *Self-Portrait* which also embraced sly cracks at numbers by the Everly Brothers plus semi-instrumentals of easy-listening bent and further lazy originals. Later that year, *New Morning* wasn't vintage Dylan either.

In the patchy early Seventies too, his only novel, *Tarantula,* was published, and he had a go at movie acting as "Alias" in 1973's *Pat Garrett And Billy The Kid,* for which he composed incidental music and the moving 'Knockin' On Heaven's Door'.

A more consistent return to form came with *Planet Waves* and 1975's

Blood On The Tracks as well as spin-off concert albums from treks like the Rolling Thunder tour which traversed North America with an itinerary publicized only locally. With Dylan and assorted guest celebrities such as Ringo Starr and Joan Baez, this jaunt was also the source of 1976's *Desire* (his last US chart-topper), scenes in Dylan's self-financed *Renaldo And Clara* film, and the *Hard Rain* television special.

Projects since have not been greeted as momentously, though Dylan continued to confound expectations with born-again Christianity pervading *Slow Train Coming,* shades of jingoism on 1983's *Infidels,* a link-up with the Grateful Dead, membership of the Traveling Wilburys, 1992's all-acoustic *Good As I Been To You* and, more blatantly asking for trouble, an earlier film role (*Hearts Of Fire*) as an ageing pop idol. What do such follies matter? The repercussions of Dylan's Sixties records resound still, having gouged so deep a wound in pop that whatever their maker gets up to in the years left to him is barely relevant.

PINK FLOYD

PSYCHEDELIC OVERLORDS

★ ★ ★

Syd Barrett *(vocals, guitar)*,
Roger Waters *(vocals, bass)*, Rick Wright *(keyboards)*,
Nick Mason *(drums)*
Formed: London, UK, 1964

Sons of Cambridge, Barrett and Waters moved to London in 1964 to begin respective courses in art and architecture. From a turnover of other student musicians, what was to become the Pink Floyd smouldered into form.

Though they started as a beat group, the gradual introduction of idiosyncratic self-composed material and lengthy monochordal extrapolations put them in a favourable position to become popular entertainers in London's "underground" clubs where light shows were among aids used to simulate psychedelic experience as the Pink Floyd, adventurous if technically limited, played on and on—and on—for tranced hippies and whirling dancers with eyes like catherine wheels.

Snapped up by EMI, their first 45, 'Arnold Layne', was, as expected, self-consciously "weird"—and a UK Top 30 entry, despite airplay restrictions. The follow-up, 'See Emily Play', climbed to Number 6

Piper At The Gates Of Dawn, their album début, was penned almost entirely by the charismatic Syd who was already proving ill-equipped to cope with the demands of pop stardom. In 1968 a second guitarist, Dave Gilmour, was brought in, and 2 months later, Barrett was out.

He managed two solo albums before effectively retiring as a professional musician and going back to Cambridge. Mention of Barrett still brings out strange stories of what people claim they saw and heard of him since his departure from Pink Floyd—the "the" had been dropped—who, if happier as concert performers, were initially at a loss without his creative input.

After the transitionary *Saucerful Of Secrets,* which included Barrett leftovers, they coped by incorporating increasingly more splendid audiovisual effects into an otherwise immobile stage act. Moreover, though individual members were competent songwriters, the stylistic emphasis on record became similar to that on the boards in that it was almost the sound at any given moment that counted rather than separate pieces. This reconciled easily with the requirements of the group's third album, 1969's *More,* a movie soundtrack. More diverting was *Ummagumma,* a double LP, half of which embraced "live" versions of tried-and-tested numbers, the

Pink Floyd in 1967. Clockwise from left: Roger Waters, Nick Mason, Rick Wright and (seated) Syd Barret.

remaining needle-time being divided in four so that solo whims could be indulged.

Waters went further in this respect by collaborating with electronics boffin Ron Geesin on incidental music to 1970's *The Body*. Geesin was to contribute to the Floyd's ambitious *Atom Heart Mother* on which quirky instrumentals and frail vocals were beefed up with brass, woodwinds and a choir.

Atom Heart Mother was also the small beginning of the Floyd's enormous success in North America. Yet, though *Obscured By Clouds* crept into *Billboard*'s Top 50, no one could have foreseen the millions that 1973's *Dark Side Of The Moon* would sell or the years it would linger in the US chart after falling from Number 1. A near-impossible market yardstick for any band, it was followed two years on by *Wish You Were Here* which, unlike *Dark Side Of The Moon*, topped the British LP list.

By comparison, *Animals* was a slow moment commercially but momentum was restored with 'Another Brick In The Wall (Part 2)', one of 26 tracks composed by Roger Waters for the robustly anti-militaristic *The Wall*.

As Pink Floyd's self-appointed boss, Waters also took most of the artistic responsibility for what he understood was to be the final Pink Floyd album (1983's *The Final Cut*). However, his legal proceedings to dissolve the group proved ineffectual, and Gilmour and Mason, with Wright among highly waged helpmates, continued to fly the Pink Floyd flag with 1987's *A Momentary Lapse Of Reason*, and a 2-year world tour that more than recouped its expensive overheads.

Enraged, Waters countered with *Radio KAOS*, an album presented in concert like an actual radio broadcast. Grander still was Roger's 1990 exhumation of *The Wall* as a televised extravaganza from Berlin with star guests and a symphony orchestra to remind the world of his Pink Floyd connection and how much that rival organization's rise to global celebrity was thanks to his leadership.

ELVIS PRESLEY

THE ONCE AND FUTURE KING

★ ★ ★

Singer
Born: January 8, 1935, Tupelo, Mississippi, USA
Died: August 16, 1977, Memphis, Tennessee, USA

BOTH THE FIGUREHEAD AND *ÉMINENCE GRISE* OF ROCK'S SHORT HISTORY, ELVIS AARON PRESLEY WAS FROM A WHITE RURAL BACKGROUND BUT SPENT MOST OF HIS ADOLESCENCE IN THE BLUFS CITY OF MEMPHIS. THOUGH SINGING IN PUBLIC WAS SECOND NATURE TO HIM, HIS WAS NOT A PARTICULARLY FLAMING YOUTH, AND HE DIDN'T RESENT HAVING TO DO A STOLID RUN-OF-THE-MILL JOB TO KEEP ALIVE.

In 1954, he joined a queue at Sun, a minuscule local studio, that offered record-your-voice facilities. Nineteen-year-old Elvis was going to sing an Ink Spots number to his own guitar accompaniment as a birthday present for his mother. His voice reached the ears of Sun's proprietor, Sam Phillips, who heard the money-making "white man who could sing the blues" that he'd despaired of ever finding.

After Presley's first release, a version of 'That's All Right', a blues by Arthur Crudup, muscled in at Number 3 in the C&W chart, further such triumphs made him the talk of the Deep South. The hillbilly-blues shout-singing of "this unspeakably untalented, vulgar young entertainer" (as a television guide would describe him) was less of an issue than his lurid dress sense, the contradiction of a girly cockage with sideburns to the ear lobes, and truculent sensu-

ality at concerts that stopped just short of open riot.

He was noticed by Hank Snow's manager, Colonel Tom Parker, who persuaded Phillips to auction Presley's Sun contract to the mightier RCA in November 1955. A few months later, the boy committed himself formally to Parker for life—and beyond.

His RCA début, 'Heartbreak Hotel', topped the US pop list, and international success followed immediately. Whether elaborated rockabilly like 'Hound Dog' and 'Jailhouse Rock' or the sulky crooning of 'Love Me Tender' or 1957's 'Don't', each new 45 sold a million regardless, giving the now wealthy Presley a splendid certainty about everything he did or said. Branching out into films—mostly with musical interludes—he proved a better actor than most pop stars who fancy themselves as cinema attractions, though the quality of his movies would so deteriorate that, after 1958's *King Creole*, each succeeding effort was usually more vacuous and streamlined than the one before.

His records inclined the same way. The turning point had been a compulsory spell in the US Army from which he was demobbed in 1960 as a sergeant and "all-round entertainer". The taming of Presley was epitomized by Italianesque warblings and infrequent self-mocking rockers, as if he was obliged to humour his old following while at the same time smirking at those of Frank Sinatra's "Rat Pack" who'd guested on his homecoming television spectacular from Miami. This

On August 16, 1977, record store windows everywhere bloomed with the King's splendour.

was one of his last performances before retiring from the stage for nigh on 8 years. All fans knew of him then was what they saw in *Kid Galahad, Paradise Hawaiian Style* and all the rest of them, plus tales of much the same veracity as those surrounding Howard Hughes.

In 1968, he returned to the stage via a television special. With rock 'n' roll revival in the air, he donned black biker leathers and concentrated on Fifties items. If rejuvenated, Elvis displayed little liking for all but the most conservative post-Beatles rock culture.

In an astounding letter to President Nixon in the early Seventies, he asked to be enrolled as a Federal Agent in order to combat "the hippie element" but, oblivious to their idol's reactionary leanings, Led Zeppelin, various Beatles and others who epitomized all that he evidently loathed would worm their way backstage to pay respects when Elvis began touring again. He'd give 'em the good old good ones but his *modus operandi* was now mostly country-pop—'There Goes My Everything', 'Polk Salad Annie' *et al*—and bursts of jingoism like 'American Trilogy'. Many were recorded in grandiose but self-indulgent cabaret which betrayed hints of the demons tormenting him in private life. Prey to obesity and hypochondria, his reign was drawing to a close.

He died on August 16, 1977. The morning after, record store windows bloomed with his splendour. For the rest of the year, he was never off Top 40 radio as he swamped the charts with five or six repromoted discs at a time. Though he'd shed the bulk of his artistic load by 1960, he'd left such an indelible impression on the complacency of post-war pop that his own later capitulation to it was shrugged off as the prerogative of stardom. Though the world became wiser to his weaknesses, the myth of his omnipotence was such that adoration has yet to dwindle for countless devotees for whom the King continues to rule from the tomb.

109

THE ROLLING STONES

THE MEN, THE MYTH, THE MAGIC

★ ★ ★

Mick Jagger *(vocals)*,
Brian Jones *(guitar)*, Keith Richards *(guitar)*, Ian Stewart
(piano), Bill Wyman *(bass)*, Charlie Watts *(drums)*
Formed: London, UK, 1962

WHEN THEY MADE THEIR STAGE DÉBUT IN 1962, THEY WERE LED BY JONES TO WORK THE UK HOME COUNTIES BLUES CLUB CIRCUIT. BY SPRING 1963, THE OUTFIT WERE HAVING MUCH THE SAME EFFECT ON THEIR AUDIENCES AS THE BEATLES HAD HAD ON THEIRS IN LIVERPOOL.

With both R&B credibility, teen appeal and a clever manager in Andrew Oldham, their cash flow was such that Wyman was able to think of packing in his day job as a storekeeper, and Jagger of not finishing his degree course in economics.

Their début 45, 'Come On', caused the *New Musical Express* to describe them as "a London group with the Liverpool sound". Just before a television début to plug the disc, Stewart was reduced to the rank of glorified road manager as he did not fit the long-haired, unkempt, rebel image that Oldham had in mind for the Stones after a necessary period of conformity in uniform stage costumes.

Only the most free-spirited teenager would dare admit finding the Stones' androgeny transfixing as a story filtered round provincial Britain that Jagger was to undergo a sex-change operation so that he could wed one of the others. This tale was undercut by those about the group's casual and unchallenging procurement of sexual gratification from female admirers. More verifiable were reports that only fire hoses could quell the tumult at their recitals. The trials of various personnel for "insulting behaviour" and drugs offences were yet to come.

For many, the Beatles had "matured" too quickly and would be soft-shoe shuffling before you could blink, but on the other side of the same coin were the Stones who'd *never* be invited to appear on any *Royal Variety Show*. Both acts were on such terms of fluctuating equality that for weeks in 1964, the Stones' fourth single, 'It's All Over Now', and the Beatles' 'A Hard Day's Night' monopolized the first two positions in the UK chart. Each listened hard to the other's latest release. The Beatles, for instance, noted Richards' use of the foot-operated fuzz-box for the riff central to 1965's '(I Can't Get No) Satisfaction'—the Beethoven's Fifth of rock—while their competitors proved just as prone to bandwagon-jumping with Jones's masterful sitar *obligato* on their third domestic Number 1, 'Paint It Black'.

Some pundits felt that the Stones had swum out of their depth with 1967's psychedelic *Their Satanic Majesties Request*. More commensurate with their return to touring after a long lay-off was 'Jumping Jack Flash' and *Beggar's Banquet,* Brian's last album before he was asked to leave by Jagger and Richards who, as the Stones' Lennon and McCartney, had snatched control of the group's destiny from him.

With new boy Mick Taylor, the Stones hosted a free concert in London's Hyde Park that served as a memorial for Jones who'd drowned two days before. On a US tour a few months later, they responded to accusations of over-charging with another buckshee bash, at Altamont, near San Francisco. This altruism, however, backfired through poor organization and a fatal stabbing yards from the stage.

Back home, the demands of the Inland Revenue drove them to tax

The Rolling Stones in 1964—with Brian Jones gazing symbolically skywards.

havens in France where they recorded *Exile On Main Street,* a double album that, for whatever reason, has been generally recognized—particularly in the USA—as the Stones' finest collection. Concentrating on the possible, it marked time artistically, as did subsequent offerings which drew lyrically from old ideas, and musically from the eternal verities of Jagger's singing, Richards' forceful rhythm, Wyman's stark throb and Watts's economic rataplans. In 1974, Taylor was replaced by Ron Wood (ex-Faces).

Their absence from the UK chart in 1977 was critical ammunition for certain quarters of the music press who, waxing sycophantically about the glories of punk, damned the Stones with faint praise without acknowledging their precedents of outrage. This storm was weathered, however, as the group carried on with much the same sort of music they'd played since the early Seventies. On the boards, ambles down Memory Lane were spiced

with more recent smashes like 'Start Me Up' and a 1986 revival of Bob and Earl's 'Harlem Shuffle'. Nevertheless, Jagger was as poutingly athletic as ever and the band still made a glorious row.

Of late, the most interesting Stone to a nosy world has been Wyman through his troubled espousal to teenager Mandy Smith—and a no-stone unturned autobiography. In 1993, he was in the news again, having announced his resignation from the group.

111

THE SEX PISTOLS

NICE LADS REALLY

★ ★ ★

Johnny Rotten *(vocals)*, Steve Jones *(guitar)*,
Glen Matlock *(bass)*, Paul Cook *(drums)*
Formed: London, UK, 1975
Disbanded: Los Angeles, US, 1978

IN THE MID-SEVENTIES, THERE WAS A LONDON CLOTHES SHOP CALLED SEX—FORMERLY LET IT ROCK—WHICH SOLD GARMENTS TAILORED BY VIVIENNE WESTWOOD, GIRLFRIEND OF ITS PROPRIETOR MALCOLM MCLAREN, WHO WAS ALSO INTERESTED IN A REHEARSING POP OUTFIT WHICH CONTAINED COOK, JONES (THEN SINGER), MATLOCK AND GUITARIST WARWICK NIGHTINGALE.

As well as a few self-composed pieces, their repertoire embraced approximations of unfashionable Sixties beat group numbers and items by the likes of the Stooges and, once managed by McLaren, the New York Dolls.

McLaren saw at least Doll-sized potential in them, as long as they got rid of uncharismatic, bespectacled Nightingale, moved Jones to guitar, and found a vocalist who needn't be a Scott Walker as long as he had the right "attitude". Eventually, McLaren and his boys stumbled upon a suitable front man in Rotten.

With a wardrobe bespoken by Sex, and as the sole clients of McLaren's newly formed Glitterbest management firm, the quartet—as the Sex Pistols—became available for bookings in 1976. As their name cropped up most in media features about the new "punk" movement, they drew much unsolicited attention from record companies.

Like Andrew Oldham had with the Rolling Stones, McLaren welcomed headline-hogging boorishness from his charges. This precipitated the swift termination of contracts with EMI and then A&M, but not before EMI had put out a début single, 'Anarchy In The UK', and both labels had allowed Glitterbest to keep the considerable advances. Before the Pistols were signed next by Virgin, an investment magazine in sardonic mood hailed them as "Young Businessmen Of The Year".

A second 45, 'God Save The Queen'—a withering blast at the royal family—almost topped the domestic charts at the height of the sovereign's Silver

Jubilee celebrations. Though heard on the recording, Matlock had been superseded by Sid Vicious whose dubious musicianship had been less important to McLaren than his assault on a rock journalist who had merited Glitterbest's displeasure.

With two comparatively non-confrontational 1977 singles, 'Pretty Vacant' and 'Holidays In The Sun',

the public seemed to have got over the initial shock of the Sex Pistols, even accepting them as a tolerable if unsavoury part of the national furniture. Predictably, the group thought up an outrageous title, *Never Mind The Bollocks, Here's the Sex Pistols,* for their first album, and inserted some swear-words in the lyrics of the few tracks that hadn't previously been issued as singles.

The end was in sight after a nerve-wracking US tour and the consequent firing of Rotten who (assisted by Virgin) instigated legal action to freeze Glitterbest's finances, but not before McLaren *in extremis* had hired Great Train Robber Ronald Biggs as lead vocalist on Pistols sessions for 'No One Is Innocent' and 'Belsen Was A Gas'. Both ditties were designed to touch up the group's reputation for outrage but were no more than self-parody.

Their rise and disintegration was chronicled on celluloid in 1979's The *Great Rock 'N' Roll*

In September 1978, Sid Vicious (far left) moved to New York where he recorded a posthumously-released in-concert album, *Sid Sings.*

Swindle, a kind of subjective *A Hard Day's Night.* One of its musical interludes was a 'My Way' sung by Vicious during his descent into an abyss of heroin addiction. Indeed, before the movie's general release, an injudicious shot of the drug brought about his death while awaiting trial for murder.

With punk but a memory, Cook and Jones made little cultural impact with post-Pistol projects. Rotten had better luck as one of Public Image Ltd, but by 1992 they were without a recording deal. The most staggering survival of all is Vivienne Westwood, who as an Eighties giant of *haute couture,* has been decorated by the Queen.

In 1992, 'Anarchy In The UK' was back in the British Top 40 as a trailer for *Kiss This,* a Sex Pistols "best of" album compiled by the original personnel. Stray paragraphs in the press nudged forward the unlikely notion of a regrouping with a reinstated Matlock who, in 1989, had published an account of his tenure with the band. Rotten's side of the story was still in preparation in 1993.

THE LEGENDS OF ROCK

THE YARDBIRDS

GOLDEN EGGS
★ ★ ★

Keith Relf *(vocals, harmonica)*,
Anthony Topham *(lead guitar)*, Chris Dreja *(rhythm guitar)*,
Paul Samwell-Smith *(bass)*, Jim McCarty *(drums)*
Formed: London, UK, 1962
Disbanded: Luton, UK, 1968

THE NURTURED PROWESS OF THREE OF THEIR FIVE LEAD GUITARISTS
HELPED MAKE THE YARDBIRDS ONE OF THE MOST INNOVATIVE ROCK
GROUPS OF THE SIXTIES. SUPERSEDING TOPHAM IN 1962, ERIC
CLAPTON WAS NO MORE ELOQUENT AN INSTRUMENTALIST BUT HAD A
STRONGER STAGE PRESENCE. A BLUES PURIST, HE LEFT FOR JOHN
MAYALL'S BLUESBREAKERS JUST BEFORE THE RELEASE OF THE YARDBIRDS'
THIRD SINGLE, MILLION-SELLING 'FOR YOUR LOVE'.

Classic Yardbirds. Left to right: Keith Relf, Chris Dreja,
Jim McCarty, Paul Samwell-Smith (back) and Jeff Beck.

Respected session musician Jimmy Page (the group's first choice as replacement) recommended Jeff Beck who had a more adventurous style than Clapton, as shown in his hand in 'Heart Full Of Soul', 'Evil-Hearted You' and further Yardbirds hits.

In 1966, Samwell-Smith left and Page agreed to play bass until Dreja was able to take over. Beck and Page then functioned as joint lead guitarists until the former went solo after a harrowing US tour.

With an increased stake in the Yardbirds' ebbing fortunes, Page suggested the hiring of mainstream pop producer Mickie Most (as Beck had done) for the records that preceded the group's final performance.

In 1968 too, Cream with Clapton, drummer Ginger Baker and bass guitarist Jack Bruce managed a more premeditated disbandment. Clapton was then railroaded into Blind Faith before throwing in his lot with the less illustrious Delaney and Bonnie And Friends.

Meanwhile, guided by Most, Beck had entered the UK Top 40 thrice with the singalong 'Hi Ho Silver Lining', 'Tallyman' and schmaltzy 'Love Is Blue'. The lead vocal on 'Tallyman' was shared with Rod Stewart who Beck, a hesitant singer, had enlisted into the Jeff Beck Group for an outstanding US concert début.

The Beck outfit's *Truth* LP—and tracks from the Yardbirds' valedictory *Little Games*—were repertory blueprints for Page's New Yardbirds, renamed Led Zeppelin for an eponymous début album that had them stereotyped as the ultimate heavy metal band.

Page had less to prove than Clapton who on his first solo LP, *Eric Clapton*, either couldn't or wouldn't be as flashy as before. Neither was he ready to function outside the context of a group—thus his subsequent *de jure* leadership of Derek And The Dominoes, who split as Eric's heroin addiction worsened in ratio to an infatuation with George Harrison's wife Patti, the muse for Clapton's 'Layla' signature tune.

Though his drug dependency persisted past the mid Seventies, his previous reputation was sufficient to put *461 Ocean Boulevard* and other lack-lustre albums into the charts. Beck too had been off the air owing to the sundering of his original group and a recovery from a serious road accident. He led another band for two albums before linking up with the Vanilla Fudge's Tim Bogart and Carmine Appice. However, this promising trio petered out mostly through lack of new material and Beck's growing dislike of heavy metal.

With Beck out of the running, Led Zeppelin ruled US stadium rock even when they retired from the road for over a year before a world tour to promote their sixth album, 1975's *Physical Graffiti*.

Beck's offering that year was *Blow By Blow* with session musicians and arrangements by George Martin. He'd become so captivated by jazz-rock that, declining a post with the Stones, he next recorded *Wired* with former Mahavishnu Orchestra keyboard-player Jan Hammer, with whom he undertook a US tour from which he surfaced as one of few rock guitarists who could handle "fusion" music convincingly. By contrast, Clapton's reassuringly more ordinary albums continued to be bought by the kind of consumers for whom the information that a favoured act's latest is just like the one before is praise indeed.

Led Zeppelin saw out the Seventies with big-selling records too. Yet, after drummer John Bonham's passing in 1980, they broke up for all practical purposes, other than rare one-off reunions.

After 1980's *There And Back* with Hammer, Beck's *Flash* was more in keeping with passing trends. Then came a liaison with Malcolm McLaren on *Waltz Darling*, and the much more characteristic *Jeff Beck's Guitar Workshop*.

In 1983, he had assisted on the only album by A Box Of Frogs, an ensemble containing Dreja, McCarty and Samwell-Smith with another singer filling in for Relf who died 7 years earlier. Since then, Beck, Page and Clapton have been among spectators during the on-going residency of McCarty's R&B band (which, until 1991, included Topham) in a London pub.

FRANK ZAPPA

MOTHER SUPERIOR

★ ★ ★

Singer/Guitarist/Composer
Born: December 21, 1940, Baltimore, Maryland, USA

AS PROPRIETOR OF A CALIFORNIAN RECORDING STUDIO IN THE EARLY SIXTIES, ZAPPA MINISTERED TO HUNDREDS OF COMMISSIONED RECORDINGS WHILE SPECULATING IN LOW-BUDGET MOVIES AND ONE-SHOT SINGLES, MULTI-TRACKED AND RELEASED UNDER A PSEUDONYM— AS WAS, FOR EXAMPLE, THE HOLLYWOOD PERSUADERS' 'TIJUANA SURF'/'GRUNION RUN' WHICH TOPPED THE MEXICAN CHARTS.

Through the medium of a vice squad *agent provocateur*, he was jailed in 1962 for "conspiracy to commit pornography". Further ethical clashes with authority came after his formation in 1964 of the Mothers Of Invention with members of the Soul Giants, a Los Angeles R&B outfit.

It was the group's submission to composer, guitarist and occasional singer Zappa's masterplan that guided them eventually to a qualified prosperity, but the Mothers' projection of themselves as freaks led the public to believe that everything they recorded was somehow a joke. However, though their *raison d'être* was often centred on comedy, they weren't the same as Freddie and the Dreamers.

They might even have been Art. Concerts and, later, albums resembled pop-Dada aural junk-sculptures made from an eclectic heap that, laced with outright craziness, included Fifties pop of the shooby-doo-wah variety, jazz, schmaltzy showbiz evergreens and the new tonalities of composers such as Stravinsky, Varese and Webern. However, Zappa's intense interest in national politics and concern over social issues was never so stifled by burlesque that it couldn't be taken seriously.

Though the Beatles had lent an investigative ear to the Mothers' first two albums, *Freak Out!* and *Absolutely Free*, their Paul McCartney had been flummoxed when Zappa rang to ask him if the Mothers could send up the *Sgt. Pepper* cover for *We're Only In It For The Money,* their first US chart entry, and a companion album to *Lumpy Gravy,* a Zappa solo curiosity, blending loaded dialogue and stubbornly chromatic passages with hummable, lushly orchestrated tunes.

Back with the Mothers, 1968's *Uncle Meat* was taped during the same block-booked sessions as *Cruising With Ruben And The Jets* which, as the antiquated *alter ego* implies, was an exercise in collaging clichés, albeit with fierce state-of-the-art jamming as its coda, and the usual subtle quotes from modern classical music.

Too clever for the commonweal, the now greatly augmented Mothers were disbanded in 1970 by Zappa who then issued an infinitely more commercial solo album than *Lumpy Gravy* in *Hot Rats,* a demonstration of his fretboard dexterity as well as the differing skills of guest performers like Captain Beefheart and violinist Jean-Luc Ponty, both of whom would join others of equally high calibre in Zappa touring bands in the Seventies.

Via a rapid turnover of personnel and style, Zappa's records came to attract, for better or worse, a wider audience in their drift towards lavatorial humour. This strain was lamentably palpable in *200 Motels,* his only major film, which, while praised for its pioneering visual effects, was blighted by a fragile plot and Frank's affrays with his co-director. It faded swiftly from general circulation, to be shown occasionally only in earnest film clubs and alternative cinemas.

An attempt in 1971 to stage *200 Motels* in London was thwarted when the Crown forced its cancellation on grounds of its sexual content. In one of the city's auditoriums that year, a "fan" hurled Zappa into the pit, confining him to a wheelchair for almost a year, during which time he produced *Waka/Jawaka* and *The Grand Wazoo,* consisting mostly of big-band instrumentals, as well as continuing to edit for release a portfolio of recordings dating back to the "Grunion Run" days.

Like Bob Dylan, Zappa racked up heftier sales achievements in the decades after he'd made his most far-reaching artistic statements. For the rest, the lyrical wit of this active anti-censorship campaigner grew coarser, and was often sung to apposite arrangements that disguised beautiful melodies. Simultaneously, Zappa went some way towards establishing himself as a composer in the same league as Varese and other of his old idols, and as a professional politician. Unimaginable though it might have been in the *Freak Out!* era, the Czech government made

Relax girls—he's married.

Zappa its official Trade and Culture Emissary in 1990, and he was considering standing for the US presidency when cancer was diagnosed. He was, nevertheless, hopeful of attending 1992's European première of a piece he'd written for Germany's Ensemble Moderne chamber group.

ADAM AND THE ANTS

KINGS OF THE WILD FRONTIER

CBS, 1980

BY 1981, ADAM ANT HAD SEIZED UPON A NEW SOUND THAT WAS PARTLY HIS OWN INVENTION, PARTLY VIA THE PROMPTING OF MALCOLM MCLAREN whose latter-day managerial clients, Bow Wow Wow—containing three ex-Ants—were less successfully incorporating into their output the abundance of Third World music that McLaren had found in public domain archives.

Behind a lead vocal that was often purest Bow Bells, the Ants stirred up a stylistic cauldron of West African tribal ceremonials—neo-military cross-rhythms and *basso profundo* chanting—war-party whooping, and metallic guitar reverberation, reminiscent of the Shadows.

While this made a most attractive noise, the group weren't a one-trick pony. 'Don't Be Square (Be There)' was a try at riffing James Brown-style that didn't quite work. More agreeable—and more original—'Jolly Roger' was Gilbert and Sullivan boiled down to four chords. This came to the notice of the West End producer of *The Pirates of Penzance* who supplicated Adam to take the starring role of 'Frederick'.

Setting them further apart were lyrics that embraced outmoded beatnik slang, jargon from spaghetti westerns and Native American lore. As you'd expect from those tracks linked conceptually to buccaneers and barbarians, violent death was a constant possibility: one minute dodging bullets in 'Los Rancheros', next, prey for "the murder-happy characters" in 'Making History'—then walking the plank in the piratical 'Jolly Roger'.

Adam decided against playing the pirate chief of light opera, but that the punk who became the schoolgirls' darling had even been considered for the part was seen as a final damnation by inverted snobs already blinded to the artistic qualities of *Kings Of The Wild Frontier* since its three singles ('Dog Eat Dog', 'Antmusic' and the title number) reached the UK Top 10, and it continued a sojourn of over a year in the album chart.

THE BEACH BOYS

LITTLE DEUCE COUPE
CAPITOL, 1963

R OCK ALBUMS *CIRCA* 1962–3 SERVED MOSTLY AS SINGLES CHASERS, TESTAMENTS TO COMMERCIAL PRAGMATISM RATHER than quality. *Little Deuce Coupe* came out just 2 months after the Beach Boys' third LP, *Surfer Girl*. Furthermore, they had the nerve to include no less than four reissued tracks; one of them from *Surfer Girl*. Nevertheless, endearingly naive as it

seems compared to *Pet Sounds*, 'Good Vibrations' *et al*, the Beach Boys' "car album" contains the same raw ingredients as those cleverer works in its attention to detail on zestful instrumental arrangements, played mainly by the Boys themselves rather than by the top Hollywood session musicians that producer Brian Wilson would employ for later discs. More crucial were the interlacing vocal harmonies on such as the sole non-original tune, Bobby Troup's 'Their Hearts Were Full Of Spring', but re-written here as 'A Young Man Is Gone', an *a capella* eulogy to James Dean that proved Brian a capable wordsmith. Wittier and more erudite lyrics by others about fuel-injected Stingrays, 409 Chevrolets and the like were also coalesced musically by Brian's lively composer mind, albeit one pressured by investors who saw the Beach Boys as a perishable commodity.

That *Little Deuce Coupe* stayed in the US chart for nearly a year implied more intrinsic strengths than the outfit's looks and personality. Almost despite themselves, the

Beach Boys had come up with a rounded entity via a bunch of songs all about automobiles, apart from the high school anthem 'Be True To Your School', and even that drops in a line about hot-rods. From lauding the record-breaking 'Spirit Of America' to weeping over 'Old Betsy', maybe one oil-change away from the breaker's yard, Brian Wilson had the craze covered. The first concept album or what?

THE BEATLES

SGT. PEPPER'S LONELY HEARTS CLUB BAND
PAROLOPHONE, 1967

L IKE BILL HALEY'S 'ROCK AROUND THE CLOCK', IT WAS JUDGED TO BE SOME SORT OF MILESTONE. "IT WAS A MILESTONE and a millstone in music history", qualified George Harrison. "There are some good songs on it but it's not our best album."

The Word made vinyl in the comfort of your own home, many, especially in the States, listened to the Beatles' latest gramophone record in the dark, at the wrong speeds, backwards and even normally. Every inch of the cover and label was scrutinized for concealed *communiqués*. By 1969, for instance, clues traceable to *Sgt. Pepper* would support a widespread and gruesome rumour that McCartney had been beheaded in an auto accident and replaced by a *doppelgänger*.

With Paul and producer George Martin as prime movers, the album had been conceived as a continuous "work" with no spaces between songs, but though it did contain various cross-fades and links, only at the beginning and near the end were you reminded of what was supposed to be Sgt. Pepper's show. "It was as if we did a few tracks", explained Starr, "and suddenly there was a fire and everyone ran out of the building but we carried on playing." Technically, it improved on 1966's *Revolver*, creating, said Harrison, "new meanings on old equipment".

Ten hours—the time spent recording the group's first LP—was no longer considered adequate for one *track* by 1967. Soon every other group was demanding the same, but not every other group had a multi-million seller that vied with their most recent 45 ('All You Need Is Love') to top the Australian singles chart. Fittingly, its 'A Day In The Life' epilogue was also the valedictory spin on Britain's pirate Radio London when it went off the air in August 1967. This was but one incident that would tie *Sgt. Pepper* forever to the psychedelic times past that it had unquestionably inspired.

DAVID BOWIE

LOW
RCA, 1977

I T WAS ALMOST LIKE A MIS-PRESSING THAT HAD STUCK TOGETHER A SIDE EACH FROM TWO MARKEDLY DIFFERENT DISCS. ON the first of these, sandwiched between two instrumentals were a handful of sketchy pop songs, such as the Top 10 single 'Sound And Vision', where Bowie made no attempt to hide his cribbing from the likes of the Yardbirds (in 'What In The World'), Mantovani ('Sound And Vision') and dear old Anthony Newley ('Be My Wife'). Oddly, it didn't matter. It was almost the point, as were impassive lead vocals floating effortlessly over the backing, but failing to mitigate the wracked drawn-curtain menace of the lyrics.

Bowie's inability to stray far beyond his central two octaves reinforced a charm peculiar to certain singers who warp a limited range to their own devices—and a similar technique was applied here to percussion. As Ringo Starr's blanketed tom-toms on Beatles albums had been in the mid-Sixties, the corrupted snare-drum sound on *Low* was so widely syndicated that studio engineers grew weary of being asked to duplicate it.

Not a solitary paradiddle was heard on *Low's* second half. The bold antithesis of punk—much in vogue that year—it consisted of the murki-

est mood music yet recorded. Its precedents included the Germanic rock of Tangerine Dream, Kraftwerk and their splinter groups, and *No Pussyfooting* by Brian Eno with King Crimson's Robert Fripp. The latter album so captivated Bowie that he called upon Eno's assistance for *Low* to such a degree that the former Roxy Music catalyst was co-writer of 'Warszawa', a ponderous outpouring of post-war desolation with

Bowie cantillating in an imaginary tongue over a stately organ-dominated track that satisfied his "emotive, almost religious" specifications.

When it was first released, you either liked *Low* or you didn't. Of two reviews in the *New Musical Express,* one reviled it as "an act of hate" while the other thought it "the first modern rock 'n' roll album". Such critiques were all the more piquant with the prior knowledge that it was recorded in a complex near the Berlin Wall—because, expounded David, "I wanted to go somewhere where I felt an alien where I didn't know the people, and where I felt in conflict. I write better like that."

THE BYRDS

THE NOTORIOUS BYRD BROTHERS
CBS, 1968

THE RECORDING OF THE NON-ORIGINAL 'GOIN' BACK'—ALSO THE SPIN-OFF 45—WAS SEEN AS A BACKWARDS STEP BY DAVE Crosby who left the group before the sessions. With Hillman the main advocate, The Byrds were to regress even more during the country-rock phase that followed, even hinting at it in the album's very title and its boots-and-saddles cover portrait.

Though Hillman and McGuinn's 'Old John Robertson' was a borderline case, there was little yee-hah exuberance in the content of *The Notorious Byrd Brothers* which, while satisfying ears conditioned to uplifting and melodic harmonies over fretboard jingle-jangling, extended the group's stylistic and technical boundaries with McGuinn's hiring of one of the first monophonic Moog synthesizers to lend contrasting sparkles to 'Space Odyssey'—a cosmic meditation—and the short but blissful sea-idyll 'Dolphins Smile'. Alternate bars of different time signatures add a less tangible poignancy to 'Get To You' in which love is all the deeper for arriving late.

Other lyrical matters include the effervescent but destructive effects of amphetamine sulphate ('Artificial Energy'), and yearning for lost childhood ('Goin' Back'). Topical then but carrying enduring weight, 'Draft Morning' was a reaction to the conscription of US youth to do their bit against the Vietcong.

Like a couple of other tracks, 'Draft Morning' had been co-written by Crosby who may have considered his exit timely after the album barely scraped into its Top 50. Commercially, it was the worst period since the Byrds started. In an industry where sales figures are mistaken for arbiters of quality, a record's artistic worth can be disregarded in accounts ledgers, on computer run-offs and during board meetings, even one with the class of *The Notorious Byrd Brothers*.

CAPTAIN BEEFHEART AND HIS MAGIC BAND

TROUT MASK REPLICA
STRAIGHT, 1969

THE FRONT COVER OF THIS DOUBLE ALBUM PORTRAYED BEEFHEART · WEARING A TOP-HAT WITH A SHUTTLECOCK BALANCED on it, and an actual trout mask replica—altogether, a most ludicrous sight. As for the music, was it mindless rubbish or a *Rolling Stone* critic's "most important work of art ever to appear on a record"?

It would not do to start a crash-course in pop with *Trout Mask Replica*, even if the arrangements dovetailed as tightly as those of a Broadway musical to accommodate Beefheart's word-play and free-form honking. On 'Ant Man Bee', he blew two saxophones at once over a jolting rhythm. A remaindered Mothers Of Invention instrumental underscored 'The Blimp', an alarming tale of a portentous figure roaming the countryside for human prey. Elsewhere, an impoverished Beefheart procrastinated over taking a hammer to a 'China Pig'—while more mordantly surreal came the likes of 'Pachuco Cadaver' and 'Bill's Corpse'.

As producer, Frank Zappa kept it rough and ready with tape clicks and extraneous mutterings quite audible. Before transferring to an orthodox studio, the dramatis personae favoured the *in situ* ambience of the secluded house where they'd rehearsed for months after Beefheart, allegedly, composed all 28 selections on a piano in a matter of hours.

THE CRAMPS

SONGS THE LORD TAUGHT US
ILLEGAL, 1980

TO THIS "GOTHIC PUNK" OUT-FIT'S LONG-TIME FANS, THE NASCENT VISION ENCAPSULATED ON *SONGS THE LORD TAUGHT US* faded swifty. The first time was the only time, for, while neither the album nor its singles made the charts, the ensemble's engagements came to be filled to overflowing principally by curiosity-seekers with only the vaguest notion about the music they'd paid to see. The Cramps were exposed as being no more scary than a ride on a fair-ground ghost train, but once they'd been as much "the real thing" as the Sex Pistols, one of few other legitimate challengers for the title of "The Last Rock 'n' Roll Group".

Because they dispensed with bass guitar, many believed there was something missing from the music—and that the players themselves were a cent short of a dollar too. You could understand this attitude when listening to Lux Interior carrying melodies mostly in a fluttering *wella-wella-wella* vibrato. This was embroidered with a bug-eyed vocal arsenal ranging from blood-curdling foghorn bass to insane falsetto, and myriad yelps *en route*. Getting more frenzied during, say, 'Rock On The Moon' or 'The Mad

Daddy', he evoked not so much some forgotten rockabilly singer than a depraved Lonnie Donegan.

The rest delivered a tuned-up and studio retractable version of the stage act. Even without the indifference towards tonality and resulting stomach-churning dischords, *Songs The Lord Taught Us* still conveyed the required good-bad rawness in its collision of rockabilly and psychedelia with a dash of T Rex.

THE CRICKETS

THE CHIRPING CRICKETS

CORAL, 1958

HOLLY AND THE CRICKETS' CORPORATE CAREER HAD LIFT-OFF WITH 1957'S 'THAT'LL BE THE DAY'. SELECTED FOR THE group's first album, this Number 1 plus follow-up hits, 'Oh Boy!' and 'Maybe Baby', were composed by members of the group and producer Norman Petty. Each demonstrated how rock 'n' roll could be

simultaneously forceful and romantic. Moreover, it didn't have to be complicated. Most Cricket originals were inspired doctorings of R&B style clichés as shown by 'Not Fade Away', built round Bo Diddley's trademark shave-and-a-haircut-six-pence rhythm

The Chirping Crickets includes two items co-written by Roy Orbison. While 'You've Got Love' is a medium-paced jollity whose title said it all, the slower 'An Empty Cup (And A Broken Date)' was an early appearance of the spurned suitor who would turn up in 'Cryin'', 'It's Over' and other million-sellers that lay ahead for Roy. Unlike these, however, 'An Empty Cup' betrays unconscious humour when a stood-up youth has been dejected further after his date "drove by with another guy". His banal contemplation that "just like this Coke, my love is gone" courts derisive sniggers rather than commiseration.

In less doleful mood, the Crickets run through three recent smashes by black R&B stars without making fools of themselves. Yet, more intense than gut-wrenching, if Holly broke sweat on, for example, Shorty Long's 'Rock Me My Baby', sonorous backing harmonies from his colleagues kept him cool so that the song could surge to a climax all the more rewarding for the restraint that preceded it.

DAVE CLARK FIVE

SESSION WITH THE DAVE CLARK FIVE

COLUMBIA, 1964

S URPRISINGLY SOPHISTICATED, NEVER DID THIS ALBUM APPROACH THE CRASH-BANG-WALLOP OF THE FIVE'S BEST-REMEMBERED singles. It was as if it had to be proved that they could hit you with the quality stuff too, for rather than being rushed through one-take stand-bys from the stage act, Clark— everything record label executives then expected a good beat group leader to be—was allowed more studio freedom than any other British pop artist of the day.

Rumours abounded that Dave didn't actually beat the skins on his own discs, but, if substitutes were ever needed, it might have been because he was required at the mixing desk.

Kicking off with an alternate mix of the rhetorical 'Can't You See That She's Mine'—the most recent smash—the Five present a stylistic diversity then unexpressed by any of their contemporaries including the Beatles and Rolling Stones. Ranging from folky 'Can I Trust You' to Cannonball Adderley-tinged jazz in 'Time', other outstanding originals include 'Funny' and 'I Love You No More'. As well as remarkable interpretations of 'On Broadway' and 'Zip-A-Dee-Doo-Dah', the depth of sound achieved on 'Rumble' exceeds the Link Wray original.

Despite a lapse into cinema interlude musak on 'Theme Without A Name', instrumentals were often their most attractive medium, and, but for the beat boom, the Five might have developed into one of the great English instrumental acts like the Tornadoes or Shadows.

It was said that if anyone criticized his music, Clark would justify himself by pulling out a wad of banknotes. Inevitably, his commercial opportunism, particularly in the USA, led to many frankly substandard releases, but *Session With The Dave Clark Five* is not one of them.

BOB DYLAN

HIGHWAY 61 REVISITED

CBS, 1965

H OWEVER STRONG *HIGHWAY 61 REVISITED* IS MUSICALLY, IT LIVES IN ITS WORDS WHICH, MORE SO THAN THE PRECEDING *BRINGing It All Back Home*, anticipated the search for profundities in pop ditties that was already elevating ephemera to Holy Writ. Though you'd have to look far for a Trogg-ologist, there was a certain New Yorker whose obsessive analysis of Dylan's lyrics was such that, in order to prove a theory about 'Desolation Row'—the album's—he placed a "wanted" ad in

BOB DYLAN HIGHWAY 61 REVISITED

a New York underground newspaper for a Dylan urine sample.

Since 1964, our hero had been singing stridently through his nose of less wistful topics than war being wrong. The nature of the new topics was inexact, especially on *Highway 61 Revisited* where the lyrics seemed to be rhymed continuations of his surreal sleeve-notes and recent press conferences where daft questions were traded for dafter answers. What are your songs about? Some of them are about 5 minutes long.

'Desolation Row' clocked in at 11 minutes 18 seconds. Like the other tracks, there was critical debate over whether its incongruous connections (e.g. 'Einstein disguised as Robin Hood') were veiled but oracular messages or else merely psuedo-cryptic words strung together to fit the tune. Naturally, Dylan inclined towards the former. Of Mr Jones, main character in 'Ballad Of A Thin Man', he insisted 'You know him but not by that name. It's a true story.' Whatever their depth, Dylan's lines were often hilarious, as in the first verse of 'Highway 61 Revisited' itself, concerning a jive-talkin' Abraham's aborted sacrifice of Issac not in biblical Moriah but—you guessed it—Highway 61.

THE MOTHERS OF INVENTION

WE'RE ONLY IN IT FOR THE MONEY
VERVE, 1968

THE CONTENT OF *WE'RE ONLY IN IT FOR THE MONEY* WASN'T FOR EVERYONE BUT, EVEN IN ABSOLUTE TERMS, IT WAS THE most perfectly produced Sixties rock album in Zappa's balance of masterful tape editing, clean sound, taut instrumental precision and premeditated carelessness.

If not for the same reasons as, say, 'Sugar Sugar', it was as instantly absorbable, mainly through being one of the funniest pop records ever released. On first encounter, it seemed like a spoof of *Sgt. Pepper's Lonely Hearts Club Band* from its sleeve montage to the 'Day In The Life' piano omega. Yet there were no laughs at all in 'Mom And Dad' when composer Zappa took a gentle tone with the "plastic" adults

interrupted certain tracks. You could also spot witty examples of what Frank called his "conceptual continuity": a vignette from the preceding *Absolutely Free* LP turns up on the vocal coda in the reprise of 'What's The Ugliest Part Of Your Body?', and, not so subtly, a string passage from 'Mother People' was repeated in *Lumpy Gravy,* the album yet to come, a less catchy illustration of Zappa's well-founded opinion that "it is theoretically possible to be 'heavy' and still have a sense of humour"

indifferent to the police turning their guns on some hippies until the revelation that their daughter was among them. The Mothers also sang of concentration camps in 'Concentration Moon', and advised reading Franz Kafka's *In The Penal Colony* prior to hearing 'The Chrome-Plated Megaphone Of Destiny', the album's challenging finale.

Beyond hitting its social and cultural targets close to the bull's-eye, some of the tunes will stay in listeners' heads unto the grave. Often just as irresistible were tiny nuances of the dialogue that both segued and

ROY ORBISON

MYSTERY GIRL
VIRGIN, 1989

DURING INTERVIEWS JUST PRIOR TO HIS SUDDEN DEATH, ROY HAD MUSED THAT HIS BEST RECORDS WERE YET TO COME—AND YOU can see his point when listening to *Mystery Girl*. His singing has all the virtues and some of the faults of a virtuoso performance, but at least it was an artist doing something he was

good at, even if he was too old to learn new tricks. In the forefront of voluminous sleeve credits was the Electric Light Orchestra's Jeff Lynne, then much in demand since producing George Harrison's *Cloud Nine* come-back. Likewise, *Mystery Girl*—and its soft-focus publicity shots—brought much of the aura of a fresh sensation to those young enough not to have heard of Roy Orbison before.

Perhaps Orbison's strongest 1980s offering, Elvis Costello's 'The Comedians', spirals thrice from a rapping spare drum to a surging drench of strings as Roy conducts himself with shocked dignity in the teeth of a dirty trick at a funfair whereby he is left dangling at the top of a ferris wheel by an operator whose donkey-jacketed virility has bewitched Roy's grounded girlfriend.

While accepting assistance from other comparative newcomers such as U2 (on 'She's a Mystery To Me') and his composer son Wesley ('The Only One'), Orbison did not renege on his past, decanting into the *Mystery Girl* cauldron a concoction with old songwriting partner Bill Dees.

Further tracks are also affiliated to some aspect of the Orbison mythology. As well as dream references in 'She's a Mystery To Me', 'In The Real World' and 'Dream You', love is lost in lush 'A Love So Beautiful' and found in 'You Got It', while 'Careless Heart' has Roy attempting to make the same amends as in 1963's 'Falling'. If far apart geographically, 'Blue Bayou' and 'California Blue' are both home thoughts from abroad. Yet the *Mystery Girl* numbers are not devalued by these comparisons. Like all Orbison's greatest work, none are so "modern" that they'll sound dated by the turn of the century.

PINK FLOYD

PIPER AT THE GATES OF DAWN
COLUMBIA, 1967

T O THE BEATLES' ANNOY-ANCE, THE PINK FLOYD WERE CONDUCTED IN FROM THE ADJACENT STUDIO TO SEE THE MASTERS AT work on *Sgt. Pepper's Lonely Hearts Club Band*. Irritation became contrition when behind the young group ambled their producer, Norman Smith. Though the protection of the Beatles' much-liked former engineer made them feel less like gatecrashers, after a few sheepish hellos, the Floyd shuffled out.

Yet the Beatles were to return the call on hearing reports on the otherworldly sounds emitting from Smith's four-track lair. Could it be that the Floyd were achieving what they were still chasing? After all, Syd Barrett—their biggest asset and biggest liability—had been glimpsing at the eternal virtually from the beginning: no smashing out 'I Saw Her Standing There' in the fleshpots of Hamburg for him. Syd hardly bothered with boy-meets-girl ditties at all. With the other personnel keeping pace, he'd gone far into the cosmos and back on 'Astronomy Domine', and disconnected with Earth altogether on 'Interstellar Overdrive'. Moreover, 'Gnome', 'Matilda Mother', 'Flaming' and his medieval 'Scarecrow' had cornered pop's gingerbread castle hour more effectively and instinctively than had 'Lucy In The Sky With Diamonds'.

The only *Piper At The Gates Of Dawn* track not composed by Barrett, 'Take Up Thy Stethoscope And Walk', existed only in its riff. Therefore, when no longer passive vehicles for his ideas, his confrères built initially on the precedent of the outer space etheria of 'Interstellar Overdrive', open-ended 'Pow R. Toc H' improvisation and the collage that ended 'Bike' rather than compete against the Beatles by developing the ground-breaking songwriting methodology that had been born of Barrett's inner chaos.

THE ROLLING STONES

AFTERMATH
DECCA, 1966

I MPRESSED WHEN LENNON AND McCARTNEY COM-PLETED 'I WANNA BE YOUR MAN' VIRTUALLY ON THE SPOT WHILE LOOK-ing in on a Stones rehearsal in 1963,

Jagger and Richards had a go at songwriting too. A year after their first A-side ('The Last Time') for the group, they were confident enough to compose all 14 tracks on the *Aftermath* album.

Jagger and Richards were not particularly receptive to the compositions of colleagues—notably Wyman and Jones. However, it was the latter's weaving of quaint instrumentation into the fabric of the *Aftermath* material that gilded many tracks with an ear-catching extraneousness. While Brian fiddled about with whatever weird implement was lying about the studio, not so esoteric were other *Aftermath* touch-ups like the 'Oi!' cadence of 'Mother's Little Helper', and a Beach Boys-type backing vocal to 'What To Do'. 'Stupid Girl' had an air of Manfred Mann about it, 'High And Dry' was virtually skiffle, and 'Goin' Home' was a blues jam that filled 12 minutes of *Aftermath's* not inconsiderable length.

Nevertheless, such artistic borrowing was usually to add icing to what were already strong songs that dwelt frequently on unexpected subjects. 'Mother's Little Helper', for example, was an enduring scrutiny of the habit-forming tablets which hasten a frantic housewife's "busy dying day". Riding rough-shod over mitherings about its sexual arrogance, 'Under My Thumb' was still in the concert set 15 years later. Of many *Aftermath* covers, 'Take It Or Leave It' gave the Searchers their final Top 40 entry, and Jagger protégé Chris Farlowe had a UK Number 1 in 1966 with the much-revived 'Out Of Time'.

ROXY MUSIC

STRANDED
ISLAND, 1973

IT WAS NAMED AFTER 'DO THE STRAND', THE PREVIOUS ALBUM'S MOST POPULAR NUMBER. THERE WAS, HOWEVER, NOTHING so immediately catchy on *Stranded*, which was also the first Roxy Music record without Brian Eno. Though Bryan Ferry was still the acme of elegance, image alone couldn't sustain this third album if his compositions were weak. Because they weren't, it wasn't necessary to blind listeners with Eno-esque science. Sonic detail came forth only after repeated listenings—a castanet clack here, a guitar shifting in and out of reverberation there. Yet the raw material didn't take as long to "grow on you". For a start, there was the British hit single 'Street Life', which, absorbing aspects of both Tamla Motown and the Rolling Stones, was intended specifically to crack the US market, but that wouldn't come until 1975's 'Love Is The Drug'.

The tracks that followed 'Street Life' relied more on reference points tangential to rock. 'Sunset', for one, was a worthy approximation of the black lyrical thrust of Jacques Brel's 'Le Moribund' in its gathering of final thoughts as death creeps nearer. Another *chansonnier* Charles Aznavour made a more tangible entrance in 'A Song For Europe', which closed with Ferry breaking into muttered Latin and then dramatic French.

With Manzanera and Mackay receiving co-writing credits, the subsequent reduction of Roxy Music to merely Ferry's accompanists was not perceptible on *Stranded*, a UK chart-topper—their first—for nearly 2 months. The follow-up, *Country Life*, rehashed some of its melodies and ideas as Ferry became smothered by cliché.

TRAFFIC

JOHN BARLEYCORN MUST DIE!
ISLAND, 1970

PROBABLY THE MOST MEMORABLE POST-BLIND FAITH TRAFFIC RECORDING, THE TITLE SONG RATHER OVERSHADOWED ITS companion tracks, which veered towards medium tempo interspersed with clever dynamic changes. Not significantly "poetic", the lyrics sidestepped much of the corny pretension of later releases.

As it would always be with Steve Winwood, the music was stronger than the words. The first half of 'Glad'/'Freedom Rider' managed without any. An attractive opening number, it made earlier Winwood instrumentals—with both Traffic and the Spencer Davis Group—seem positively throwaway.

This album rose swiftly to Number 11 in the UK chart. Considering that Traffic had been on ice for a year, this was good going—though, reduced once more to a trio, substantial overdubbing was still necessary to realize an orchestration of up to eight instruments.

The sparsest arrangement was reserved for 'John Barleycorn' itself, which was one of these numbers that are "worth the whole price of the album". A turntable fixture at the group's cottage had been an *a capella* rendition by the Watersons, a family from Hull. Traffic exchanged their modal harmonies for guitar, unobtrusive percussion, flute interludes and one-finger piano—and Steve's understated vocal was further from Ray Charles than any 1965 Spencer Davis Group fan could ever have imagined.

THE UNITED STATES OF AMERICA

THE UNITED STATES OF AMERICA
CBS, 1968

A FEATURE IN BRITAIN'S *INTERNATIONAL TIMES* UNDERGROUND NEWSPAPER HAD THIS AMONG THE FOUR ESSENTIAL albums that every rock fan should own.

Virtually all that is known of the group is that they were New Yorkers, and that after disbanding in 1969, leader Joseph Byrd, backed by the Field Hippies, recorded *The American Metaphysical Circus*. Other than that, the United States Of America simply came and went, and in between they recorded an eyestretching LP that was an aesthetic as well as an intellectual experience—a kind of fusion of John Cage and Lennon-McCartney.

Their *modus operandi* was not so much tampering with the workings of instruments with, say, effects pedals, as actually utilizing electronically generated sound. Often only the drums put their music in the realms of pop at all. However, running a gamut from pseudo-horrific flash to subdued ghostliness, the tape collages and electronic twiddling went past mere gimmickry to be as integral to the lyrics and melodies, filtered mostly through Dorothy Moscowitz's clear soprano, as the common chord. Yet, when reduced to the acid test of just voice and piano, the songs stood tall.

THE VELVET UNDERGROUND

THE VELVET UNDERGROUND AND NICO
VERVE, 1970

T HE LIKES OF 'SUNDAY MORNING' AND 'I'LL BE YOUR MIRROR' WERE ALMOST ORTHODOX LOVEY-DOVEY POP BUT the group's canon contained more intriguing stabs at sado-masochism ('Venus In Furs') and drug addiction ('I'm Waiting For The Man', 'Heroin') in which a sense of longing rather than denigration took tangible form as literary-musical wit from one who was assumed to live the part, for composer Reed as a Seventies solo performer would get out a syringe to simulate the process of mainlining during 'Heroin', a substance he would later say he'd never touched. The observations of others repudiated this claim.

The loudest ovations would be reserved for 'Heroin' and other tracks from the beginning of Reed's tenure with the Velvet Underground, encapsulated on an album more influential than any he'd issued since, on which the impromptu was prized more than technical accuracy—with some numbers underlined not with a bass guitar but a noisy electronic drone that made a melodrama from what had once been a presence rather than a sound on Sixties vinyl.

While the album peaked at a wretched Number 171 in the US chart, it was, with the Mothers Of Invention's *Freak Out!*, perhaps the most stunning début by any North American rock act, even if, just prior to its release, its makers had been dismissed as "decadent" by a West Coast media pundit bedazzled by flower-power. Recorded mostly in colder New York, *The Velvet Underground And Nico* had little space for any fashionable travesty of love.

SCOTT WALKER

CLIMATE OF HUNTER
VIRGIN, 1984

T HE FORMER WALKER BRO-THER'S SELF-PENNED *SCOTT 4* COULD NOT BE MADE TO SUIT 1969'S CHARTS ANY MORE THAN his next solo album, *Climate Of Hunter*, could in a later pop generation. Indeed, *Scott 4* and its creator's composing talents went unnoticed by the general public for years until the interest of sagacious acts like Ultravox and David Bowie sparked a spate of belated and mostly hollow praise in the music press.

Unlike *Nite Flights*, *Climate of Hunter* contains less emphasis on melodic construction and verse-chorus ditties than the overall development of a wracked, menacing mood via a wry, abstract lyricism and aptly bleak arrangements with a small ensemble instead of the orchestras of yore.

In the unlikely event that we hear no more of Scott Walker, *Climate Of Hunter* stands as a strange but worthy epitaph. One reviewer described its content as 'the most terminal songs ever written'—and you can understand why While Tennessee Williams's 'Blanket Roll Blues' is the only non-original, most of Scott's own *lieder* have numbers rather than names—even the spin-off 45 'Track 3'. It's just as well with some of them—especially 'Track 7', which has the enigmatically mournful title 'Stump of a Drowner'. Yet, because it's Scott Walker and not Extreme Noise Terror or Napalm Death singing, it's not the musical equivalent of a video nasty—and, as it

sold only a few thousand copies, it might even be Art.

THE YARDBIRDS

YARDBIRDS
COLUMBIA, 1966

MANY TRACKS ON THE YARDBIRDS' FIRST STUDIO ALBUM SHOWCASED JEFF BECK. YET BECK'S PLAYING HAS TENDED to displace other personnel's more discreet innovations, such as an anticipation of the pastoral lyricism and acoustic determination of post-Yardbirds' projects like Renaissance and Stairway, perhaps Britain's best-loved New Age ensemble.

The Yardbirds' studio time was always limited. However, although they were granted 5 days off from a punishing schedule to record *Yardbirds,* any extension may have detracted from the proceedings' spontaneity and endearing imperfections. Certainly no cover or revival—whether Paul and Barry Ryan's 'I Can't Make Your Way' or

even Stairway's 'Turn Into Earth'—has ever surpassed the Yardbirds' blueprint.

'We'd start with a basic rhythm and bass pattern, and then . . . sort of build it up', elucidated Jim McCarty with particular reference to the self-composed collection's 45 'Over Under Sideways Down'. Generally, while the rest organized the backing, Keith Relf was elsewhere collating the words, though certain items belonged to individual Yardbirds, such as the elegiac 'Turn Into Earth', brainchild of co-producer Paul Samwell-Smith.

If able to continue in a recognizable form, the outfit never really recovered from Paul's departure a month before the album's release. The subsequent attention given fretboard god Beck also contributed to the group's self-destruction, but when working according to each member's capacity on *Yardbirds,* they were at their most effective as one of what an otherwise disgruntled ex-manager, Simon Napier-Bell, would admit were "four rock bands in the world that really counted".

CD listings

The following list contains the main releases by the artists and bands described earlier in the book. The artists and bands are listed alphabetically, followed by their albums (also in alphabetical order). Each entry contains the name of the album and the year of original release, followed by the record labels and catalogue numbers under which the albums have been released in CD format.

Some albums are currently unavailable on CD.

ACE
The Best Of Ace *1987*
UK: SEE FOR MILES: SEECD 214
US: SEE FOR MILES: SF-214

BRYAN ADAMS
Bryan Adams *1987*
UK: A&M: CDA3100
US: A&M: CD69902
Cuts Like A Knife *1983*
UK: A&M: CDA4919
US: A&M: CD69981
Into The Fire *1987*
UK: CDA 3907
US: A&M: VPCD-6907
Reckless *1985*
UK: A&M: CDA 5013
US: A&M: CD5013
Waking Up The Neighbours *1991*

UK: A&M: 397164-2
US: A&M: CD5367
You Want It You Got It *1985*
UK: A&M: CDA 3154
US: A&M: CD69955

ANIMALS
The Complete Animals *1991*
UK: EMI: CDEM 1367
The EP Collection *1988*
UK: SEE FOR MILES: SEECD 244
US: SEE FOR MILES: SF-244
Trackin' The Hits *1991*
UK: CHARLY: CDLIK 72

B52s
B52s *1986*
UK: ISLAND: IMCD-1

US: WARNER BROS: 3355-2
Cosmic Thing *1989*
UK: REPRISE: 925854-2
US: REPRISE: 25854-2
Mesopotamia *1982*
UK: ISLAND: IMCD-107
US: WARNER BROS: 3641
Wild Planet *1980*
UK: ISLAND: IMCD-108
US: WARNER BROS: 3471

SYD BARRETT
Barrett *1971*
UK: EMI: CDP 746606-2
US: CAPITOL: C21Y-46606
Crazy Diamond *1993*
UK: EMI: 7805572
The Madcap Laughs *1970*
UK: HARVEST: CDP 746607-2
US: CAPITOL: C21Y-46607
Opel *1988*
UK: HARVEST: SHSP 4126
US: CAPITOL: C11G-91206

BEACH BOYS
20 Golden Greats *1987*
UK: EMI: CDEMTV 1
US: CAPITOL: 521H-46738
Beach Boys' Concert/Live In London *1965/1971*
UK: CAPITOL: CDP 7936952
US: CAPITOL: 4N-16134
Beach Boys' Party!/Stack-O-Tracks *1966/1966*
UK: CAPITOL: CDP 7936982
US: CAPITOL: C2-93698
Endless Summer *1987*
UK: EMI: CDP 7464672

US: CAPITOL: C22S 46467
Friends/20-20 *1968/1969*
UK: CAPITOL: CDP 7936972
US: CAPITOL: C21S-93697
Little Deuce Coupe/All Summer Long *1963*
UK: CAPITOL: CDP 7936932
US: CAPITOL: C21Z-93693
Made In The USA *1986*
UK: CAPITOL: CDEN 5005
US: CAPITOL: C22S-46324
Pet Sounds *1966*
UK: CAPITOL: CDP 7484212
US: CAPITOL: C21S-48421
Smiley Smile/Wild Honey *1967/1968*
UK: CAPITOL: CDP 7936962
US: CAPITOL: C21Z-93696
Spirit Of America *1987*
UK: CAPITOL: CDP 7466182
US: CAPITOL: C22S-46618
Summer In Paradise *1992*
UK: BROTHER: BBR 727-2
US: BROTHER: 727
Surfer Girl/Shut Down (Vol 2) *1963/1963*
UK: CAPITOL: CDP 7936922
US: CAPITOL: C21Z-93692
Surfin' Safari/Surfin' USA *1962/1963*
UK: CAPITOL: CDP 7936912
US: CAPITOL: C21S-93691
Today/Summer Days (And Summer Nights) *1966/1966*
UK: CAPITOL: CDP 7936942

US: CAPITOL: C21S-93694

BEATLES
Abbey Road *1969*
UK: EMI: CDPCS 7088
US: CAPITOL: C21Z-46446
The Beatles *1968*
UK: EMI: CDS 7464438
US: CAPITOL: C22V-46443
Beatles For Sale *1991*
UK: EMI: CDP 7464382
US: CAPITOL: C21S-46438
A Hard Day's Night *1964*
UK: EMI: CDP 7464372
US: CAPITOL: C21Z-46437
Help! *1965*
UK: EMI: CDP 7464392
US: CAPITOL: C21S-46439
Let It Be *1970*
UK: EMI: CDPCS 7096
US: CAPITOL: C21S-46447
Magical Mystery Tour *1968*
UK: EMI: CDPCTC 255
US: CAPITOL: C21Z-48062
Please Please Me *1963*
UK: EMI: CDP 7464352
US: CAPITOL: C21S-46435
Revolver *1966*
UK: EMI: CDP 7464412
US: CAPITOL: C21S-46441
Sgt. Pepper's Lonely Hearts Club Band *1967*
UK: EMI: CDPCS 7027
US: CAPITOL: C21Z-46442
With The Beatles *1963*
UK: EMI: CDP 7464362
US: CAPITOL: C21S-46436

JEFF BECK
Blow By Blow *1972*
UK: EPIC: CDEPC 32367
US: COLUMBIA: WEK-33409
The Late 60s *1988*
UK: EMI: CDP /467102

**CAPTAIN BEEFHEART
AND HIS MAGIC BAND**
**I May Be Hungry
But I Sure Ain't
Weird** *1992*
UK: SEQUEL: NEXCD 215
**The Legendary
A&M Sessions** *1992*
UK: EDSEL: BLIMPCD 902
Trout Mask Replica
1969
US: WARNER: CD-02027

BEE GEES
Bee Gees 1st *1967*
UK: RSO: 825220-2
US: POLYDOR: 825220-2
**Best Of The Bee
Gees Volume 1** *1969*
UK: POLYDOR: 831594-2
US: POLYDOR: 831594-2
**Best Of The Bee
Gees Volume 2** *1970*
UK: POLYDOR: 831960-2
US: POLYDOR: 831960-2
Odessa *1969*
UK: RSO: 825451-2
US: POLYDOR: 825451-2
**Tomorrow The
World** *1992*
UK: THUNDERBOLT CDTB 135

CHUCK BERRY
The Chess Box *1989*
UK: MCA: CHC 6800001

US: CHESS: CHD3-80001
The EP Collection
1991
UK: SEE FOR MILES: SEECD 320
The London Sessions
1971
UK: CHARLY: CDRED 20
US: CHESS: CHD-9295
**Rock And Roll
Music** *1991*
UK: CHARLY: CDINS 5002
US: CHESS: PDK2-1134
**Rock & Roll
Rarities** *1991*
UK: CHARLY: CDCHESS 1005
US: CHESS: CHD-92521

DAVE BERRY
**Hostage To The
Beat** *1988*
UK: LINE: BUCD 9005430
US: LINE: BUCD 9005430

BLACK SABBATH
Blackest Sabbath
1989
UK: VERTIGO: 838818
The Eternal Idol
1988
UK: VERTIGO: VERH
US: WARNER BROS 25548-2

DAVID BOWIE
Aladdin Sane *1973*
UK: EMI: CDEMC 3579
US: RYKODISC: RCD 10135
David Bowie *1967*
UK: LONDON/DERAM:
800087-1
US: POLYDOR: 800087-2
Diamond Dogs *1974*
UK: EMI: CDEMC 3584

US: RYKODISC: RCD-10137
"Heroes" *1977*
UK: EMI: CDEMD 1025
US: RYKODISC: RCD-10143
Hunky Dory *1971*
UK: EMI: CDEMC 3572
US: RYKODISC: RCD-10133
Let's Dance *1983*
UK: EMI AMERICA:
CDP 746002-2
US: EMI AMERICA:
E21Y-46002
Never Let Me Down
1987
UK: EMI AMERICA:
CDP 746677-2
US: EMI AMERICA:
E21Y-46677
Pin Ups *1973*
UK: EMI: EMC 3580
US: RYKODISC: RCD-10136
**The Rise And Fall
Of Ziggy Stardust
And The Spiders
From Mars** *1972*
UK: EMI: EMC 3577
US: RYKODISC: RCD-10134
Tin Machine *1989*
UK: EMI AMERICA: MTS 1044
US: EMI AMERICA: E2-91990
Tonight *1984*
UK: EMI AMERICA:
CDP 746047-2
US: EMI AMERICA:
E21Y-46047

BYRDS
The Collection *1991*
UK: CASTLE: CCSCD 151
**The Notorious Byrd
Brothers** *1968*
UK: DEMON: EDCD 262

US: COLUMBIA: CK-09575
**Sweetheart Of The
Rodeo** *1968*
UK: DEMON: EDCD 227
US: COLUMBIA: WCK-9670
**Younger Than
Yesterday** *1967*
UK: DEMON EDCD 227
US: COLUMBIA: CK-09442

CANNED HEAT
**The Best of Canned
Heat** *1991*
US: EMI AMERICA:
E21Y-48377
**Boogie With
Canned Heat** *1968*
UK: SEE FOR MILES: SEECD 62
Canned Heat *1967*
UK: SEE FOR MILES: SEECD 268
Hallelujah *1973*
UK: SEE FOR MILES: SEECD 248
Livin' The Blues *1972*
UK: SEE FOR MILES: SEECD 97

ERIC CLAPTON
**The Cream Of Eric
Clapton** *1987*
UK: POLYDOR: ECTV 1
US: POLYTEL: 833519-2
Crossroads *1988*
UK: POLYDOR: 835261-2
US: POLYDOR: 835261-2

DAVE CLARK FIVE
Glad All Over Again
1993
UK: EMI: CDEMTV 75

CLIMAX BLUES BAND
**Couldn't Get It
Right** *1976*

UK: SEE FOR MILES:
SEE CD 222
US: SEE FOR MILES: SF-222
FM/Live *1974*
UK: SEE FOR MILES:
SEE CD 279
US: SEE FOR MILES: 269
**The Harvest Years
'69–'72** *1990*
UK: SEE FOR MILES: SEECD 316
Plays On *1972*
UK: SEE5: C5CD 556
US: SEE FOR MILES: 556

JOE COCKER
The Collection *1992*
UK: CASTLE: CLACD 126
The Collection 2
1992
UK: CASTLE: CLACD 304
**I Can Stand A Little
Rain** *1974*
UK: CASTLE: CLACD 144
US: A&M: CD-3175
Joe Cocker *1969*
UK: CASTLE: CLACD 236
US: A&M: CD 3326
Live In LA *1976*
UK: CASTLE: CLACD-189
Unchain My Heart
1987
UK: CAPITOL: EST 2045
US: CAPITOL: C21Y-48285
**With A Little Help
From My Friends**
1969
UK: CASTLE: CLACD 172
US: A&M: CD-3106

ALICE COOPER
**Alice Cooper Goes
To Hell** *1976*

UK: WEA 7599272992
US: WARNER BROS CD-02896
The Beast Of Alice
1991
UK: WEA K 2417812
**Billion Dollar
Babies** *1973*
UK: WEA 759927692
US: WARNER BROS CD-02685
Live In 1968 *1992*
UK: DEMON EDCD 320
**Live At The
Whiskey A-Go-Go
1969** *1992*
UK: EDSEL: NESTCD 903
US: RHINO: 70369-2

ELVIS COSTELLO
Almost Blue *1981*
UK: DEMON: FIENDCD 33
US: COLUMBIA: CK-37562
Armed Forces *1979*
UK: DEMON: FIENDCD 21
US: COLUMBIA: WCK-35709
**Blood And
Chocolate** *1986*
UK: DEMON: XFIENDCD 80
US: CBS: CK-40518
Get Happy! *1980*
UK: DEMON: FIENDCD 24
US: COLUMBIA: CK-36347
**Goodbye Cruel
World** *1984*
UK: DEMON: FIENDCD 75
US: COLUMBIA: CK-36347
Imperial Bedroom
1982
UK: DEMON: FIENDCD 36
US: COLUMBIA: CK-38157
King Of America
1986
UK: DEMON: FIENDCD: 78

US: COLUMBIA: CK-40173
My Aim Is True *1977*
UK: DEMON: FIENDCD 13
US: COLUMBIA: VCK 35037
Punch The Clock
1983
UK: DEMON: FIENDCD 72
US: COLUMBIA: CK-38897
Trust *1981*
UK: DEMON: FIENDCD 30
US: COLUMBIA: WCK-37051

CRAMPS
A Date With Elvis
1984
UK: ACE: CDWIK 46
US: ENIGMA: D21Y-73579
Look Mom No Head
1986
UK: ACE: CDWIKD 101
US: RESTLESS: 72586-2
Smell Of Female *1983*
UK: ACE: CDWIKM 95
US: ENIGMA: D21Y-73578
**Songs The Lord
Taught Us** *1981*
UK: ILLEGAL: ILPCD 5
US: A&M: 44797-0007-2

**CREEDENCE
CLEARWATER REVIVAL**
Bayou Country
1970
UK: ACE: CDFE 502
US: FANTASY: FCD-658
The Concert *1972*
UK: ACE: CDFE 511
US: FANTASY: FCD-4501
Cosmo's Factory
1970
UK: ACE: CDFE 505
US: FANTASY: FCD-608

**Creedence
Clearwater Revival**
1969
UK: ACE: CDFE 501
US: FANTASY: FCD 4512-2
Green River *1970*
UK: ACE: CDFE 503
US: FANTASY: FCD-612
Pendulum *1971*
UK: ACE: CDFE 512
US: FANTASY: FCD-4517-
**Willy & The
Poorboys** *1970*
UK: ACE: CDFE 504
US: FANTASY: FCD-613

**CROSBY, STILLS, NASH
AND YOUNG**
4 Way Street *1971*
UK: WEA: 75677824082
US: ATLANTIC: 824408-2
American Dream
1988
UK: ATLANTIC: 781888-2
US: ATLANTIC: 81888
Deja Vu *1970*
UK: ATLANTIC: K 250001
US: ATLANTIC: 19118

DEEP PURPLE
The Anthology *1985*
UK: EMI CDEM 1374
**The Book Of
Taliesyn** *1969*
UK: EMI HARVEST CDP
792408-2
Burn *1974*
UK: EMI CZ 203
US: DEEP PURPLE: 2766-2
**Come Taste The
Band** *1975*
UK: EMI CDP7940322

US: WARNER BROS 26454-2
**Deep Purple In
Rock** *1970*
UK: EMI CDFA 3011
US: WARNER BROS 01877
Fireball *1971*
UK: EMI CZ 30
US: DEEP PURPLE 2564-2
Machine Head *1972*
UK: EMI: CDFA 3158
US: WARNER BROS: 03100
**Shades Of Deep
Purple** *1992*
UK: EMI: CZ 170
Singles As & Bs *1993*
UK: EMI: CDP 7810092
Stormbringer *1974*
UK: EMI: CZ 142
US: WARNER BROS: 26456-2

DEF LEPPARD
Adrenalize *1992*
UK: PHONOGRAM: 510978
US: POLYGRAM: 512185
High 'N' Dry *1981*
UK: PHONOGRAM: 818836-2
US: POLYGRAM: 818836-2
Hysteria *1987*
UK: PHONOGRAM: 830675-2
US: POLYGRAM: 830675-1
**On Through The
Night** *1980*
UK: PHONOGRAM: 822533-2
US: POLYGRAM: 822533-2
Pyromania *1983*
UK: PHONOGRAM: 810308-2
US: POLYGRAM: 810308-2

DIRE STRAITS
Alchemy *1984*
UK: VERTIGO: 818243-2
US: POLYDOR: 818243-2

Brothers In Arms
1985
UK: VERTIGO: 824499-2
US: WARNER BROS: 25264-2
Communique *1983*
UK: VERTIGO: 800052-2
US: POLYDOR: 800052-2
Dire Straits *1983*
UK: VERTIGO: 800051-2
US: WARNER BROS: 3266-2
Love Over Gold
1983
UK: VERTIGO: 800088-2
US: WARNER BROS: 3266-2
Making Movies *1983*
UK: VERTIGO: 800050-2
US: POLYDOR: 800050-2

LONNIE DONEGAN
The Collection *1992*
UK: CASTLE: CCSCD 223
The EP Collection
1992
UK: SEE FOR MILES: SEECD 346
The Originals *1992*
UK: SEE FOR MILES: SEECD 331

DOORS
Alive She Cried
1983
UK: ELEKTRA: 960269-2
US: WEA: CD-60269
**The Best Of The
Doors** *1991*
UK: WEA: K 9603452
US: ELEKTRA: 60345
The Doors *1967*
UK: ELEKTRA: K 242012
US: ELEKTRA: 74007-2
LA Woman *1971*
UK: ELEKTRA: K 242090
US: ELEKTRA: 75011-2

Live At The
Hollywood Bowl
1987
UK: ELEKTRA: 960741-2
Morrison Hotel *1970*
UK: ELEKTRA: K 242080
US: ELEKTRA: 75007-2
Strange Days *1968*
UK: ELEKTRA: K 242016
US: ELEKTRA: 74014-2
Waiting For The Sun
1968
UK: ELEKTRA: K 242041
US: ELEKTRA: 74024-2

BOB DYLAN
Biograph *1991*
UK: SONY: 66509
US: SONY: C3K-38830
Blonde On Blonde
1966
UK: SONY: 22130
US: COLUMBIA: CD-22130
Blood On The
Tracks *1975*
UK: COLUMBIA: 69067
US: COLUMBIA: VCK-33235
Bob Dylan *1961*
UK: SONY: 32001
US: COLUMBIA: CK-08579
The Bootleg Series
1-3, 1961-91 *1991*
UK: SONY: 4680864
US: SONY: C3K-47382
Bringing It All Back
Home *1965*
UK: CBS: 62515
US: COLUMBIA: WCK-9128
Desire *1976*
UK: CBS: 86003
US: COLUMBIA: VCK-33893
Down In The

Groove *1988*
UK: CBS: 4602672
US: COLUMBIA: CK-40957
Good As I Been To
You *1992*
UK: COLUMBIA: 4727102
US: COLUMBIA: 4727102
Greatest Hits *1967*
UK: SONY: 4609072
US: COLUMBIA: VCK-9463
Highway 61
Revisited *1965*
UK: CBS: 62572
US: COLUMBIA: WCK-9189
John Wesley
Harding *1968*
UK: CBS: 63252
US: COLUMBIA: WCK-9604
Oh Mercy *1989*
UK: CBS: 456800
US: COLUMBIA: CK-45281
Slow Train Coming
1979
UK: CBS: 86095
US: COLUMBIA: WCK-36120

EAGLES (US)
Hotel California *1976*
UK: WEA: K 253051
US: ASYLUM: 103-2
Live *1980*
UK: WEA: K 462032

FACES
First Step *1970*
UK: DEMON: EDCD 240
US: DEMON: EDCD240

GEORGIE FAME
The First Thirty
Years *1990*
UK: CONNOISSEUR: VSOP 144

FLEETWOOD MAC
Behind The Mask
1992
UK: WEA: 7599261112
US: WARNER BROS: 26111
Fleetwood Mac *1976*
UK: WEA: K 254043
US: WARNER: CD-02281
Mirage *1982*
UK: WEA: K 256952
US: WARNER BROS: 23607
The Original
Fleetwood Mac *1992*
UK: CASTLE: ESSCD 026
Rumours *1977*
UK: WEA: K256344
US: WARNER BROS: 3012-2
Then Play On *1969*
UK: WEA: K 9274482
US: REPRISE: 6368-2
Tango In The Night
1987
UK: WEA: K 9254712
US: WARNER BROS: 25471-2

FREE
Fire And Water *1970*
UK: ISLAND CID 9104
US: A&M 75021-3663-2
Free *1968*
UK: ISLAND CID 9104
Free At Last *1972*
UK: ISLAND CID 9192
Free Live *1971*
UK: ISLAND CID 9160
US: A&M 75021-4306-2
Heartbreaker *1973*
UK: ISLAND CID 9217
US: POLYGRAM 842361-2
Highway *1971*
UK: ISLAND CID 9138
Tons Of Sobs *1969*

UK: ISLAND CID 9089

GENESIS
Selling England By
The Pound/The
Lamb Lies Down On
Broadway *1973/1974*
UK: VIRGIN: TPAK 1
Shaking The Tree
1992
UK: VIRGIN: PGTVD 6
US: GEFFEN: GEFD24326-2

**GERRY AND THE PACE-
MAKERS**
The Best Of The
EMI Years *1992*
UK: EMI: CDP 7990302
The Best Of Gerry
And The
Pacemakers *1991*
US: UNITED ARTISTS: E21Y-
46583

GARY GLITTER
Greatest Hits *1992*
US: RHINO: 70729-2

GRATEFUL DEAD
From The Mars
Hotel *1974*
UK: ACE: GDCD 4007
US: GRATEFUL DEAD:
GDCD-4007
Infrared Roses *1991*
US: GRATEFUL DEAD: 4014
Steal Your Face *1976*
UK: ACE: GDCD 4006
US: GRATEFUL DEAD: 4006
Two From The Vault
1991

UK: ACE: GDCD 2
US: GRATEFUL DEAD: 4016
Workingman's Dead
1970
UK: WEA: K 246049
US: WARNER BROS: 1869-2

GUNS N' ROSES
Appetite For
Destruction *1987*
UK: GEFFEN 924148-2
US: GEFFEN GEFD 24148
GN'R Lies *1988*
UK: GEFFEN 924198-2
US: GEFFEN GEFD 24198
Use Your Illusion I
1991
UK: GEFFEN GEFD 24415
US: GEFFEN GEFD 24415
Use Your Illusion II
1991
UK: GEFFEN GEFD 24420
US: GEFFEN GEFD 24420

GEORGE HARRISON
Best of Dark Horse
1991
UK: WEA: K 9257262
US: WARNER BROS: 25726
Live In Japan *1993*
UK: WEA: 7599269642
US: WARNER BROS: 26964 2

**JIMI HENDRIX
EXPERIENCE**
Are You
Experienced? *1967*
UK: POLYDOR 825416-2
US: REPRISE RS-06261
The Concerts *1991*
UK: CASTLE: CCSCD 235
US: REPRISE: CD-22306

Cornerstones 67–70
1990
UK: Polydor: 847231

The Cry Of Love
1971
UK: Polydor 847242-2
US: Reprise CD-02034

Electric Ladyland
1968
UK: Polydor 847233-2
US: Reprise CD-06307

Radio One Sessions
1991
UK: Castle CCSCD 212
US: Rykodisc: RCD-20078

Smash Hits *1968*
UK: Polydor 825255-2
US: Warner Bros 2276-2

War Heroes
1972
UK: Polydor 847262-2

HERMAN'S HERMITS
The Best Of The EMI Years Volume 1
1992
UK: EMI: CDP 7970422

The Best Of The EMI Years Volume 2
1992
UK: EMI: CDEMS 1616

The Collection *1991*
UK: Castle: CCSCD 246

Their Greatest Hits
1990
US: Abkco: 42227-2

HOLLIES
20 Golden Greats
1978
UK: EMI: CDP 7462382
US: Capitol: CDP-46238

The EP Collection
1991
UK: See For Miles: SEECD 94
US: See For Miles: 64

Hottest Hits *1992*
US: EMI: PDK2-1041

The Other Side Of The Hollies *1991*
UK: See For Miles: SEECD 302

BUDDY HOLLY
Buddy Holly *1959*
UK: MCA: DMCL 1752
US: MCA: MCAD-25239

The Chirping Crickets *1957*
UK: Sequel: NEMCD 629
US: MCA: MCA-31182

Giant *1969*
UK: Castle: CLACD 307

Reminiscing *1963*
UK: Castle: CLACD 308
US: MCA: PDK2-1121

HUMAN LEAGUE
Dare *1992*
UK: CDV: 2192
US: A&M: 75021-4892-2

Greatest Hits *1988*
UK: Virgin: HLTV 1
US: A&M: 5227

JAN AND DEAN
Drag City *1991*
UK: C5: C5CD 560
US: See For Miles: 560

Jan And Dean Take Linda Surfing *1963*
UK: C5: C5CD 585

Little Old Lady From Pasadena *1963*
UK: C5: C5CD 574

Ride The Wild Surf
1992
UK: C5: C5CD 562

Surf City *1992*
UK: C5: C5CD 584
US: K-Tel: 665

JETHRO TULL
A Little Light Music
1992
UK: Chrysalis: CHR 1954

Live At Hammersmith '84
1990
UK: Raw Fruit: FRSCD 004

On The Crest Of A Knave *1987*
UK: Chrysalis: CDD 1590
US: Chrysalis: VKM-41590

Original Masters
1987
UK: Chrysalis: CCD 1515
US: Chrysalis: VKM-41515

Rock Island *1989*
UK: Chrysalis: CHR 1708
US: Chrysalis: F21S-21708

Stand Up! *1969*
UK: Mobile: UDCD 524
US: Chrysalis: CCD-1042

ELTON JOHN
21 At 33 *1980*
UK: Rocket: 800055-2
US: MCA: MCAD-31054

Breaking Hearts
1984
UK: Rocket: 822088-2
US: MCA: MCAD-10501

Captain Fantastic
1975
UK: DJM: CD 1
US: MCA: MCAD-31078

The Fox *1981*
UK: Rocket: 800063-2
US: MCA: MCAD-10497

Jump Up *1982*
UK: Rocket: 800037-2
US: MCA: 10499

Goodbye Yellow Brick Road *1973*
UK: DJM: CD 2
US: MCA: MCA2-6894

Greatest Hits *1974*
UK: DJM: CD 3
US: MCA: MCAD-37215

Love Songs *1982*
UK: Rocket: 810783-2

Too Low For Zero
1983
UK: Rocket: 811052-2
US: MCA: 10485

TOM JONES
Delilah *1968*
UK: London: 820486-2

The Golden Hits
1987
UK: London: 810192-2
US: Polygram: 810192-2

Green Green Grass Of Home *1967*
UK: London: 820182-2

Live In Las Vegas
1969
UK: London: 820318-2
US: Polydor: 820318-2

KINKS
Arthur *1969*
UK: Castle: CLACD 162
US: Warner Bros: 6366-2

Face To Face *1966*
UK: Castle: CLACD 158
US: Castle: CLACD-157

Kinda Kinks *1965*
UK: Castle: CLACD 156
US: Rhino: 70316-2

The Kinks *1964*
UK: Castle: CLACD 155
US: K-Tel: 3954

Live At Kelvin Hall
1966
UK: Castle: CLACD 160
US: Castle: CLACD-160

Something Else *1967*
UK: Castle: CLACD 159
US: Castle: CLACD-159

The Star Collection
1992
UK: BMG: 262 764

The Village Green Preservation Society
1968
UK: Castle: CLACD 161
US: Warner Bros: 6327-2

BILLY J. KRAMER
The Definitive Collection *1992*
US: EMI: E21Y-96055

LED ZEPPELIN
Coda *1982*
UK: Swan Song: 7900512
US: Swan Song: 90051-2

Houses Of The Holy
1973
UK: Atlantic: 250014
US: Atlantic: 19130-2

In Through The Out Door *1979*
UK: Atlantic: 259410
US: Atlantic: CD-16002

Led Zeppelin *1969*
UK: Atlantic: 240031
US: Atlantic: CD-19126

Led Zeppelin 2 *1969*
UK: Atlantic: 240037
US: Atlantic: CD-19127
Led Zeppelin 3 *1970*
UK: Atlantic: 250002
US: Atlantic: CD-19128
Physical Graffiti *1975*
UK: Atlantic: 289400
US: Swan Song: 200-2
Presence *1976*
UK: Atlantic: 259402
US: Swan Song: 8416-2
The Song Remains The Same *1976*
UK: Atlantic: 289402
US: Atlantic: CD-00201
The Symbols Album *1971*
UK: Atlantic: 250008
US: Atlantic: 19129-2

JOHN LENNON
Double Fantasy *1980*
UK: EMI: CDP 7914252
US: Capitol: C21S 91425
Imagine *1971*
UK: EMI: CDP 7466412
US: Capitol: C21S-46641
The John Lennon Collection *1982*
UK: EMI: CDP 7915162
US: EMI USA: C21S-91516
John Lennon/Plastic Ono Band *1971*
UK: EMI: CDP 7467702
US: Capitol: C21S-46770
Live In New York City *1992*
UK: EMI: CDP 7461962
US: Capitol: C21S-46196
Menlove Avenue *1981*

UK: EMI: CDP 7465762
US: Capitol: C21S-46576
Mind Games *1973*
UK: EMI: CDP 7467692
US: Capitol: C21Z-46769
Rock 'N' Roll *1975*
UK: EMI: CDP 7467072
US: Capitol: C21Z-46707
Shaved Fish *1975*
UK: EMI: CDP 7466422
US: Capitol: C21S 46642
Walls And Bridges *1974*
UK: EMI: CDP 7467682
US: Capitol: C21Z-46768

JERRY LEE LEWIS
The Alternative Collection *1992*
UK: Charly SUND 35
The Best Of Jerry Lee Lewis *1992*
UK: Music Club: MCCD 081
US: Curb: D21K-77446
The EP Collection *1991*
UK: See For Miles: 3EECD 307
Ferriday Fireball *1991*
UK: Charly: CDCHARLY 1
Honky Tonk Rock 'N' Roll Piano Man *1991*
UK: Ace: CDCH 332
Pretty Much Country *1992*
UK: Ace: CDCH 348
US: Ace: 348
Rare And Rockin' *1991*
UK: Charly: CDCHARLY 70
The Sun Years *1991*

UK: Charly: CDSUNBOX 1
US: Rhino: R11G-70255

MAMAS AND PAPAS
The EP Collection *1992*
UK: See For Miles: SEECD 333

MANFRED MANN
The Collection *1992*
UK: Castle: CCSCD 245
Manfred Mann's Earth Band 1971–1991 *1992*
UK: Cohesion: BOMMECD 1

BOB MARLEY
Exodus *1977*
UK: Island: TGLCD 6
US: Island: 846208-2
Live At The Lyceum *1981*
UK: Island: TGLCD 4
US: Island: 846203-2
Natty Dread *1975*
UK: Tuff Gong: RRCD/CT 3
US: Island: CID-9281
Rebel Music *1986*
UK: Tuff Gong: RRCD/CT 5
US: Island: CIDM-1097
Songs Of Freedom *1992*
UK: Island: TGCVX 1
The Very Best Of The Early Years *1992*
UK: Music Club: MCCD 033

PAUL McCARTNEY
Flowers In The Dirt *1989*
UK: Parlophone: PCSD 106
US: Capitol: C21S-91653

PAUL McCARTNEY and WINGS
At The Speed Of Sound *1992*
UK: EMI: CDFA 3229
US: Capitol: C21S-48199
Band on The Run *1973*
UK: EMI: CDP 7460552
US: Capitol: C21Y-46675
Venus And Mars *1975*
UK: EMI: CDFA 3213
US: Capitol: C21Y-46984
Wild Life *1971*
UK: EMI: CDFA 3101
US: Capitol: C21Y-52017
Wings' Greatest *1978*
UK: EMI CDP 7460562
US: Capitol: C21Y-46056
Wings Over America *1976*
UK: EMI: CDFA 7467158
US: Capitol: C22V-46715

MONKEES
The Collection *1992*
UK: Arista: 262507
Hey! Hey! It's The Monkees Greatest Hits *1989*
UK: K-Tel: 1432
US: Arista: ARCD-8313

MOODY BLUES
The Collection *1991*
UK: Castle: CCSCD 105
US: Castle: CCSCD-105
Days Of Future Passed *1968*
UK: Decca: 800082-2
US: Threshold: 820006

The Present *1983*
UK: Decca: 810119-2
US: Threshold: 810119-2
Sur La Mer *1988*
UK: Polygram: POLH 43
US: Polydor: 835756-2
Voices In The Sky *1986*
UK: Decca: 820155-2
US: Polydor: 820155-2

VAN MORRISON
Avalon Sunset *1989*
UK: Polydor: 839262
US: Polydor: 839262-2
The Bang Masters *1992*
UK: Sony: 4683094
US: Epic: EK-47041
The Best Of Van Morrison *1990*
UK: Polydor: 841970
US: Polydor: 841970-2
Enlightenment *1990*
UK: Polydor: 847/1002
US: Polygram: 847100-2
Irish Heartbeat with The Chieftains *1988*
UK: Mercury: MERH 13
US: Polydor: 834496-2
It's Too Late To Stop Now *1975*
UK: Polydor: 839163-2
US: Warner Bros: 02760
A Period of Transition *1977*
UK: Polydor: 839165-2
US: Warner Bros: 2987-2
Poetic Champions Compose *1987*
UK: Mercury: MERH 110
US: Polydor: 832585-2

137

Saint Dominic's Preview *1976*
UK: POLYDOR: 839162-2
US: WARNER BROS: CD-02633
Tupelo Honey *1975*
UK: POLYDOR: 839161-2
US: WARNER BROS: 1950-2
Veedon Fleece *1974*
UK: POLYDOR: 839166-2
US: WARNER BROS: 02805-2
Wavelength *1978*
UK: POLYDOR: 839169-2
US: WARNER BROS: 3212-2

MOTHERS OF INVENTION
Cruising With Ruben And The Jets *1969*
UK: ZAPPA: CDZAP 4
US: RYKODISC: RCD-10063
Freak Out! *1966*
UK: ZAPPA: CDZAP 1
US: RYKODISC: RCD-40062
Uncle Meat *1968*
UK: ZAPPA: CDZAP 3
US: RYKODISC: RCD-10064
Weasels Ripped My Flesh *1970*
UK: ZAPPA: CDZAP 24
US: RYKODISC: RCD-10163

ROY ORBISON
The Collection *1991*
UK: CASTLE: CCSCD 147
The Early Days (The Sun Years—US) *1991*
UK: CHARLY: CDINS 5010
US: RHINO: R21S-70916
Go Go Go *1991*
UK: CHARLY: CDCHARLY 27
Mystery Girl *1990*

UK: VIRGIN: V 2576
US: VIRGIN: V21Y-86103

PINK FLOYD
Atom Heart Mother *1970*
UK: EMI: CDP: 746381-2
US: CAPITOL: C2AY-46381
Dark Side Of The Moon *1973*
UK: EMI: CDP: 746001-2
US: CAPITOL: C21Z-46001
Delicate Sound Of Thunder *1988*
UK: EMI: CDEMQ 5009
US: COLUMBIA: C2K-44484
Ummagumma *1969*
UK: EMI: CDP: 746404-8
US: CAPITOL: CDPB-46404
The Wall *1979*
UK: EMI: CDP: 746036-8
US: COLUMBIA: C2K-36183

PINK FLOYD/ SYD BARRETT
More *1969*
UK: EMI: CDP: 746386-2
US: CAPITOL: C21S-46346
The Piper At The Gates Of Dawn *1967*
UK: EMI: CDP: 746382-2
US: CAPITOL: 46384
Saucer Of Secrets *1968*
UK: EMI: CDP: 746383-2
US: CAPITOL: C21S-46383

GENE PITNEY
The Best Of Gene Pitney *1969*
UK: ACE MC-ACTC 004
US: K-TEL: 3028

Big Forty *1992*
UK: CHARLY: CDINSD 5051
The Collection *1992*
UK: CASTLE: CCSCD 239
The EP Collection *1992*
UK: SEE FOR MILES: SEECD 313

POLICE
Ghost In The Machine *1981*
UK: A&M: CDA 63730
US: A&M: 3730
Outlandos D'Amour *1979*
UK: A&M: CDA 68502
US: A&M: 3311
Regatta De Blanc *1979*
UK: A&M: CDA 64792
US: A&M: 3312
Synchronicity *1983*
UK: A&M: CDA 63735
US: A&M: 3735
Zenyatta Mondatta *1980*
UK: A&M: CDA 64831
US: A&M: 3720

ELVIS PRESLEY
50,000,000 Elvis Fans Can't Be Wrong *1960*
UK: RCA: ND 89429
US: RCA: 5197-2
A Date With Elvis *1959*
UK: RCA: ND 90356
US: RCA: 2011-2
Elvis *1984*
UK: RCA: PD 81382
US: RCA: PCD1-5199

Elvis' Christmas Album (Blue Christmas—US) *1971*
UK: RCA: ND 90300
US: RCA: 9800-4-R
Elvis' Golden Records *1958*
UK: RCA: PD 85196
US: RCA: PCDI-5196
Elvis' Golden Records Volume 3 *1964*
UK: RCA: ND 82765
US: RCA: 2765-2
Elvis' Gold Records Volume 4 *1990*
UK: RCA: ND 83921
US: RCA: 1297-2
Elvis Is Back! *1960*
UK: RCA: ND 89031
US: RCA: 2231-2
Elvis NBS TV Special *1969*
UK: RCA: ND 83894
US: RCA: 61021-2
Elvis Presley *1988*
UK: RCA: ND89046
US: RCA: PCD1-5198
The Elvis Presley Sun Collection *1988*
UK: RCA: ND 89107
US: RCA: 6414-1-R12
For LP Fans Only *1961*
UK: RCA: ND 90359
US: RCA: 1990-2
From Elvis In Memphis *1969*
UK: RCA: ND 90548
US: RCA: 51456-2
His Hand In Mine *1961*

UK: RCA: ND 83935
US: RCA: 1319-2
How Great Thou Art *1967*
UK: RCA: ND 83758
US: RCA: 3758-2
King Creole *1958*
UK: RCA: ND 83733
US: RCA: 3733
Loving You *1977*
UK: RCA: ND 81515
US: RCA: 5198-2
Moody Blue *1977*
UK: RCA: ND 90252
US: RCA: 2428-2
On Stage February 1970 *1970*
UK: RCA: ND 90549
US: RCA: 54362-2

PRETTY THINGS
1967–1971 *1992*
UK: SEE FOR MILES: CM 103
Parachute *1970*
UK: DEMON: EDCD 289
SF Sorrow *1967*
UK: DEMON: EDCD 236
US: DEMON: 236

QUEEN
At The Beeb *1992*
UK: BAND OF JOY: BOJCD 001
A Day At The Races *1976*
UK: EMI: CDP 746208-2
US: HOLLYWOOD: 61035-2
Flash Gordon *1980*
UK: EMI: CDP 746214-2
US: HOLLYWOOD: 61203-2
The Game *1980*
UK: EMI: CDP 746213-2
US: HOLLYWOOD: 61063-2

Greatest Hits *1981*
UK: EMI: CDP 74603-2
Hot Space *1982*
UK: EMI: CDP 746215-2
US: HOLLYWOOD: 61038-2
Jazz *1978*
UK: EMI: CDP 746210-2
US: HOLLYWOOD: 61062-2
A Kind Of Magic
1986
UK: EMI: CDP 746267-2
US: HOLLYWOOD: 61152-2
Live Magic *1986*
UK: EMI: CDP 746413-2
US: HOLLYWOOD: 61066-2
The Miracle *1989*
UK: PARLOPHONE:
CDPCSD 107
US: HOLLYWOOD: 61234
**A Night At The
Opera** *1975*
UK: EMI: CDP 746207-2
US: HOLLYWOOD: 61065-2
Queen *1975*
UK: EMI: CDP 746204-2
US: HOLLYWOOD: 61064-2
Queen II *1974*
UK: EMI: CDP 746205-2
US: HOLLYWOOD: 61232-2
Sheer Heart Attack
1974
UK: EMI: CDP 746206-2
US: HOLLYWOOD: 61036-2
The Works *1984*
UK: EMI: CDP 7460616-2
US: HOLLYWOOD: 61233-2

LOU REED
The Bells *1992*
UK: ARISTA: 262918
Berlin *1973*
UK: RCA: PD 84388

US: RCA: 207-2
**Between Thought
And Expression** *1992*
UK: RCA: PD 90621
US: RCA: 2356
Coney Island Baby
1976
UK: RCA: PD 83807
US: RCA: 915-2
Grown Up In Public
1983
UK: ARISTA: 262 917
Magic And Loss
1992
UK: SIRE: 759926662
US: WARNER BROS:
7599-26662-2
Mistrial *1986*
UK: RCA: PD 87190
US: RCA: 7190-2
New Sensations
1984
UK: RCA: PD 84998
US: RCA: 7190-2
New York *1989*
UK: SIRE: 925829-2
US: WARNER BROS: 25829-2
**Rock 'N' Roll
Animal** *1974*
UK: RCA: PD 83664
US: RCA: 3664-2
Sally Can't Dance
1975
UK: RCA: PD 80611
US: RCA: 611-2
Songs For 'Drella
1990
UK: SIRE: WX 345
US: WARNER BROS: CD-26140
Transformer *1973*
UK: RCA: PD 83806
US: PCD1-4807

**Walk On The Wild
Side** *1987*
UK: BMG: ND 83753
US: RCA: 3753-2

REM
**Automatic For The
People** *1992*
UK: WFA: 9262-45055-2
Dead Letter Office
1987
UK: IRS: CD 70054
US: IRS: CD70054
Document *1987*
UK: IRS: DMIRG 1025
US: IRS: IRSD-42059
**Fables Of The
Construction** *1985*
UK: IRS: DMIRF 1003
US: IRS: IRSD-5592
Life's Rich Pageant
1986
UK: IRS: DMIRG 1014
US: IRS: IRSD-5783

CLIFF RICHARD
20 Golden Greats
1977
UK: EMI: CDEMTVS 6
Always Guaranteed
1987
UK: EMI: CDP 7467052
**Established
1958/The Best Of
Cliff** *1968*
UK: EMI: CDEMC 3637
**Me And My
Shadows** *1960*
UK: EMI: CDEMC 3628
**Rock 'N' Roll
Juvenile** *1979*
UK: EMI CZ 188

Wired For Sound
1981
UK: FAME: CDFA 3159

LITTLE RICHARD
22 Classic Cuts *1991*
UK: ACE: CDCH 195
US: ACE: CDCH-195
The Fabulous *1991*
UK: ACE: CDFAB 001
US: SPECIALTY: SPCD-7012-2
**His Greatest
Recordngs** *1991*
UK: ACE: CDCH 109
US: ACE: CHA-109
**Rock And Roll
Resurrection** *1991*
UK: CHARLY: CDCHARLY 84
US: SPECIALTY: VCK-40492
**Slippin Shakin' An'
Slidin'** *1991*
UK: CHARLY: CDINS 5014
**The Specialty
Sessions** *1991*
UK: ACE: ABOXCD 1
US: ACE: ABOXCD-1

ROLLING STONES
12 x 5 *1964*
UK: LONDON: 820048-2
US: ABKCO: 7402-1
Aftermath *1966*
UK: LONDON: 820050-2
US: ABKCO: 7476-1
Beggar's Banquet
1968
UK: LONDON: 820084-2
US: ABKCO: 7539-1
**Between The
Buttons** *1967*
UK: LONDON: 820138-2
US: ABKCO: 7499-1
December's

Children *1966*
UK: LONDON: 820135-2
US: ABKCO: 7451-1
**Exile On Main
Street** *1972*
UK: CBS: CDCBS 450196-2
US: COLUMBIA: 40489
Goat's Head Soup
1973
UK: CBS: CDCBS 450207-2
US: COLUMBIA: VCK-40492
**Got Live If You
Want It** *1966*
UK: LONDON: 820137-2
US: ABKCO: 7493-1
Let It Bleed *1969*
UK: LONDON: 820052-1
US: ABKCO: 8004-1
Out Of Our Heads
1965
UK: LONDON: 820039-2
US: ABKCO: 7429-1
The Rolling Stones
1964
UK: LONDON: 820047-2
US: ABKCO: 7375 1
**The Rolling Stones
Now!** *1965*
UK: LONDON: 820133-2
US: ABKCO: 7420-1
Steel Wheels *1989*
UK: CBS: 456752
US: COLUMBIA: CK-45333
Sticky Fingers
1971
UK: CBS: CDCBS 450195-2
US: COLUMBIA: VCK-40488
**Their Satanic
Majesties Request**
1967
UK: LONDON: 820129-2
US: ABKCO: 8002-1

ROXY MUSIC
Roxy Music/For Your Pleasure/ Stranded
1972/1973/1973
UK: VIRGIN: TPAK 23
Street Life (Greatest Hits) *1992*
UK: VIRGIN: EGCTV 1
The Ultimate Collection *1988*
UK: EG: EGTV 2

SEARCHERS
30th Anniversary *1991*
UK: SEQUEL: NXTCD 170
US: SEQUEL: NEXCD-170
The Best Of The Searchers *1991*
UK: PICKWICK: PWK 4076
The Complete Collection *1992*
UK: CASTLE: CCSCD 303
The EP Collection *1993*
UK: SEE FOR MILES: SEECD 275
US: SEE FOR MILES: 275
The EP Collection Volume 2 *1993*
UK: SEE FOR MILES: SEECD 359

SEX PISTOLS
The Great Rock 'N' Roll Swindle *1979*
UK: VIRGIN: CDVD 2510
Kiss This *1992*
UK: VIRGIN: V 2702
Never Mind The Bollocks *1977*
UK: VIRGIN: CDV 2086
US: WARNER BROS: 3147-2

The Original Pistols Live (Better Live Than Dead—US)
1986
UK: DOJO: DOJOCD 45
US: RESTLESS: 72255-2

SHADOWS
The EP Collection Volume 1 *1992*
UK: SEE FOR MILES: SEECD 246
US: SEE FOR MILES: 246
The EP Collection Volume 2 *1992*
UK: SEE FOR MILES: SEECD 296
From Hank Bruce Brian And John *1962*
UK: BGO: BGOCD 20
The Original Chart Hits 1960–1980 *1990*
UK: EMI EM 1354
Specs Appeal Plus *1993*
UK: EMI: CZ 514

SHANGRI LAS
Remember *1992*
UK: CHARLY: CDINS 5021
US: COLLECTABLES: 5011

SMALL FACES
The Autumn Stone *1969*
UK: CASTLE: CLACD 114
The Complete Collection *1992*
UK: CASTLE: CCSCD 302
Ogden's Nut Gone Flake *1968*
UK: CASTLE: CLACD 116
US: IMMEDIATE: 46964

The Singles As And Bs *1992*
UK: SEE FOR MILES: SEECD 293

BRUCE SPRINGSTEEN
Born In The USA *1984*
UK: CBS: CDCBS 86304
US: COLUMBIA: 38653
Born To Run *1975*
UK: CBS: CDCBS 80959
US: COLUMBIA: 33795
Darkness At The Edge Of Town *1978*
UK: CBS: CDCBS 86061
US: COLUMBIA: 35318
Greetings From Asbury Park NJ *1985*
UK: CBS: CDCBS 65480
US: COLUMBIA: 35318
Live 1975-85 *1986*
UK: CBS: CDCBS 450227-2
Nebraska *1982*
UK: CBS: CDCBS 85669
US: COLUMBIA: 38358
The River *1980*
UK: CBS: CDCBS 88510
US: COLUMBIA: 36854
Tunnel Of Love *1987*
UK: CBS: CDCBS 460279-2
US: COLUMBIA: 40999

STATUS QUO
The Collection *1992*
UK: CASTLE: CCSCD 114
The Early Works *1992*
UK: CASTLE: ESBCD 136
Spare Parts *1992*
UK: CASTLE: CLACD 206

STEELEYE SPAN
All Around My Hat *1975*
UK: BGO: BGOCD 158
US: SHANACHIE: CD-79059
The Best Of Steeleye Span *1987*
UK: CHRYSALIS: CCD 1467
The Collection *1992*
UK: CASTLE: CCSCD 292

ROD STEWART
Body Wishes *1983*
UK: WARNER BROS: 923877-2
US: WARNER BROS: CD-23877
Camouflage *1984*
UK: WARNER BROS: 925095-2
US: WARNER BROS: CD-25095-2
Every Beat Of My Heart *1986*
UK: WARNER BROS: 925446-2
US: WARNER BROS: CD-25446
Every Picture Tells A Story *1971*
UK: MERCURY: 822385-2
US: MERCURY: 82385-2
Gasoline Alley *1970*
UK: MERCURY: 824881-2
US: MERCURY: 824881-2
Greatest Hits *1979*
UK: WARNER BROS: 3373-2
US: WARNER BROS: 03373-2
Just A Little Misunderstood *1992*
UK: M CLASSICS: MCLASCD 2
Never A Dull Moment *1972*
UK: MERCURY: 826263-2
US: MERCURY: 826263-2
Out Of Order *1988*
UK: WARNER BROS: 925684-2

US: WARNER BROS: 25684-2
The Rod Stewart Album *1986*
UK: MERCURY: 830572-2
US: MERCURY: 830572-2
Sing It Again Rod *1973*
UK: MERCURY: 824882-2
US: MERCURY: 824882-2
Smiler *1974*
UK: MERCURY: 832056-2
US: MERCURY: 832056-2
Storyteller *1990*
UK: WARNER BROS: 925987
US: STIEFEL: CD25987

STONE ROSES
The Stone Roses *1989*
UK: SILVERTONE: ORECD 502
US: NOVUS: 1184-2
Turns Into Stone *1992*
UK: SILVERTONE: 0RECD 521

STRANGLERS
The Collection 1977–82 *1982*
UK: LIBERTY: CDP: 7460662
Live At The Hope And Anchor *1992*
UK: EMI: CDP 7987892
The Old Testament 1977–1982 *1992*
UK: EMI: CDSTRANG 1
The Stranglers' Greatest Hits *1991*
US: EPIC: 47081

THEM
Them Featuring Van Morrison *1991*

UK: LONDON: 8101652
US: POLYDOR: 820925-2

THIN LIZZY
BBC Radio One:
Live In Concert *1992*
UK: BBC WIN 024
The Collection *1992*
UK: CASTLE: CCSCD 117
Dedication: The
Very Best Of Thin
Lizzy *1991*
UK: VERTIGO: 848192
US: MERCURY: 848530-2

TRAFFIC
John Barleycorn
Must Die *1970*
UK: ISLAND: IMCD 40
US: ISLAND: CIDM-90058
Last Exit *1968*
UK: ISLAND: IMCD 41
US: ISLAND: 842787-2
Low Spark Of High-
Heeled Boys *1972*
UK: ISLAND: IMCD 42
US: ISLAND: CIDM-9180
Mr. Fantasy *1967*
UK: ISLAND: IMCD 43
US: ISLAND: CIDM-90060
Shoot Out At The
Fantasy Factory *1973*
UK: ISLAND: IMCDD 158
US: ISLAND: 422-842781-1
Smiling Phases *1992*
UK: ISLAND: IMCDD 158
US: POLYGRAM: 510553-2
Traffic *1968*
UK: ISLAND: IMCD 45
US: ISLAND: CIDM-90059
Welcome To The
Canteen *1971*

UK: ISLAND: IMCD 39
US: ISLAND: 422-842417-1

TROGGS
Athens To Andover
1992
UK: PAGE ONE: ESS 180
Au *1990*
UK: NEW ROSE: ROSE 186
US: CASTLE: 2615262-CD
Wild Things *1992*
UK: SEE FOR MILES: SEECD
256

TYRANNOSAURUS
REX/T REX
Beard Of Stars/
Unicorn
1970/1969
UK: CASTLE: TFOCD 15
The Collection *1992*
UK: CASTLE: CLACD 136
The Early Years *1993*
UK: DOJO: EARLD 1
Electric Warrior
1971
UK: CASTLE: CLACD 180
US: REPRISE: CD-06466

U2
Rattle And Hum
1988
UK: ISLAND: IS 400
US: ISLAND: 842299-2

VELVET UNDER-
GROUND
The Best Of The
Velvet Underground
1989
UK: POLYDOR: 841164
US: POLYGRAM: 841164-2

UNITED STATES OF
AMERICA
The United States
Of America *1992*
UK: DEMON: EDCD 233

SCOTT WALKER
Climate Of Hunter
1984
UK: VIRGIN: CDV 2303
No Regrets *1976*
UK: FONTANA: 510 831
Scott *1967*
UK: POLYGRAM: 5108792
Scott 2 *1968*
UK: FONTANA: 510 880-2
Scott 3 *1969*
UK: FONTANA: 510 881-2
Scott 4 *1969*
UK: FONTANA: 510 882-2

WALKER BROTHERS
After The Lights Go
Out *1990*
UK: FONTANA: 84283

THE WHO
The Singles *1991*
UK: POLYDOR: 8159652
Who's Better Who's
Best *1988*
UK: POLYGRAM: 835389
US: MCA: MCAD-8031

JOHNNY WINTER
The Collection *1992*
UK: CASTLE: CCSCD 167
Scorchin' Blues *1993*
UK: SONY: 4716612
US: SONY: 52466
Second Winter *1970*
UK: DEMON: EDCD 312

US: COLUMBIA: WCK-9947

STEVE WINWOOD
Arc Of A Diver *1981*
UK: ISLAND: CID 9576
US: ISLAND: CIDM-1301
Back In The High
Life *1986*
UK: ISLAND: CID 9844
US: ISLAND: CIDM-1300
Chronicles *1987*
UK: ISLAND: SSWCD 1
US: ISLAND: CIDM-1298
The Spencer Davis
Group Featuring
Stevie Winwood
1992
UK: ISLAND: IMCD 151
The Best Of The
Spencer Davis
Group *1992*
US: RHINO: RNC-70172
Steve Winwood *1977*
UK: ISLAND: CID 9494
US: ISLAND: 422-842774-1
Talking Back To
The Night *1982*
UK: ISLAND: CID 9777
US: ISLAND: CIDM-1299

YARDBIRDS
The Collection *1992*
UK: CASTLE: CCSCD 141
The First Recordings
1992
UK: CHARLY: CDCHARLY 186
US: LAND R: 4400
Five Live Yardbirds
1964
UK: CHARLY: CDCHARLY 182
US: RHINO: 70189-2
Greatest Hits *1968*

UK: CHARLY: CDCHARLY 8
US: RHINO: RNCD-75895
On Air *1991*
UK: BAND OF JOY: BOJCD 200
Over Under
Sideways Down *1991*
UK: RAVEN: RVCD 12
Yardbirds *1966*
UK: DEMON: EDCD 116

FRANK ZAPPA
Hot Rats *1970*
UK: ZAPPA: CDZAP 2
US: RYKODISC: RCD-10066

ZOMBIES
The Best Of The
Zombies (Greatest
Hits—US)
1992
UK: MUSIC CLUB: MCCD 002
US: DCC COMPACT CLASSICS:
DZC-052
The Collection *1992*
UK: CASTLE: CCSCD 196
US: CASTLE: CCSCD196
The EP Collection
1993
UK: SEE FOR MILES: SEECD 358
Meet The Zombies
1964
UK: RAZOR: CD 34
New World *1992*
UK: CASTLE: ESSCD 131
Odessey and Oracle
(sic) *1969*
UK: MUSIC MACHINE: MACD 6
US: RHINO: 70186-2
The Singles As And
Bs *1992*
UK: SEE FOR MILES: SEECD 30
US: SEE FOR MILES: 30

index

Page numbers in italics refer to captions to illustrations